SOCIAL JUSTICE

Opposing Viewpoints

SOCIAL JUSTICE

Opposing Viewpoints

David L. Bender & Bruno Leone, Series Editors

Bonnie Szumski, Book Editor
Claudia Debner, Associate Editor
Terry O'Neill, Associate Editor
Lynn Hall, Editorial Assistant
Pat Jordan, Editorial Assistant

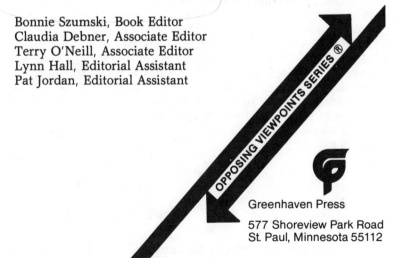

Greenhaven Press

577 Shoreview Park Road
St. Paul, Minnesota 55112

361.1
So 13

Library of Congress Cataloging in Publication Data
Main entry under title:

Social justice.

(Opposing viewpoints series)
Bibliography: p.
Includes index.
1. Social problems—United States—Addresses, essays, lectures.
2. Minorities—Civil rights—United States—Addresses, essays, lectures. 3. United States—Social policy—Addresses, essays, lectures.
I. Szumski, Bonnie, 1958- . II. Series.
HN65.S572 1984   361.1   84-13724
ISBN O-89908-348-x
ISBN O-89908-323-4 (pbk.)

"Congress shall make no law...
abridging the freedom of speech,
or of the press."

first amendment to the U.S. Constitution

The basic foundation of our democracy is the first amendment
guarantee of freedom of expression. The *Opposing Viewpoints
Series* is dedicated to the concept of this basic freedom and the
idea that it is more important to practice it than to enshrine it.

Contents

Chapter 3: Is the US Fair to Immigrants?

Chapter 4: Do Women Receive Equal Treatment?

Why Consider Opposing Viewpoints?

"It is better to debate a question without settling it than to settle a question without debating it."

Joseph Joubert (1754-1824)

The Importance of Examining Opposing Viewpoints

The purpose of the Opposing Viewpoints Series, and this book in particular, is to present balanced, and often difficult to find, opposing points of view on complex and sensitive issues.

Probably the best way to become informed is to analyze the positions of those who are regarded as experts and well studied on issues. It is important to consider every variety of opinion in an attempt to determine the truth. Opinions from the mainstream of society should be examined. But also important are opinions that are considered radical, reactionary, or minority as well as those stigmatized by some other uncomplimentary label. An important lesson of history is the eventual acceptance of many unpopular and even despised opinions. The ideas of Socrates, Jesus, and Galileo are good examples of this.

Readers will approach this book with their own opinions on the issues debated within it. However, to have a good grasp of one's own viewpoint, it is necessary to understand the arguments of those with whom one disagrees. It can be said that those who do not completely understand their adversary's point of view do not fully understand their own.

A persuasive case for considering opposing viewpoints has been presented by John Stuart Mill in his work *On Liberty*. When examining controversial issues it may be helpful to reflect on his suggestion:

> The only way in which a human being can make some approach to knowing the whole of a subject, is by hearing what can be said about it by persons of every variety of opinion, and studying all modes in which it can be looked at by every character of mind. No wise man ever acquired his wisdom in any mode but this.

Analyzing Sources of Information

The Opposing Viewpoints Series includes diverse materials taken from magazines, journals, books, and newspapers, as well as statements and position papers from a wide range of individuals, organizations and governments. This broad spectrum of sources helps to develop patterns of thinking which are open to the consideration of a variety of opinions.

Pitfalls to Avoid

A pitfall to avoid in considering opposing points of view is that of regarding one's own opinion as being common sense and the most rational stance and the point of view of others as being only opinion and naturally wrong. It may be that another's opinion is correct and one's own is in error.

Another pitfall to avoid is that of closing one's mind to the opinions of those with whom one disagrees. The best way to approach a dialogue is to make one's primary purpose that of understanding the mind and arguments of the other person and not that of enlightening him or her with one's own solutions. More can be learned by listening than speaking.

It is my hope that after reading this book the reader will have a deeper understanding of the issues debated and will appreciate the complexity of even seemingly simple issues on which good and honest people disagree. This awareness is particularly important in a democratic society such as ours where people enter into public debate to determine the common good. Those with whom one disagrees should not necessarily be regarded as enemies, but perhaps simply as people who suggest different paths to a common goal.

Developing Basic Reading and Thinking Skills

In this book carefully edited opposing viewpoints are purposely placed back to back to create a running debate; each viewpoint is preceded by a short quotation that best expresses the author's main argument. This format instantly plunges the reader into the midst of a controversial issue and greatly aids that reader in mastering the basic skill of recognizing an author's point of view.

A number of basic skills for critical thinking are practiced in the activities that appear throughout the books in the series. Some of the skills are:

Evaluating Sources of Information The ability to choose from among alternative sources the most reliable and accurate source in relation to a given subject.

Separating Fact from Opinion The ability to make the basic distinction between factual statements (those that can be demonstrated or verified empirically) and statements of opinion (those that are beliefs or attitudes that cannot be proved).

Identifying Stereotypes The ability to identify oversimplified, exaggerated descriptions (favorable or unfavorable) about people and insulting statements about racial, religious or national groups, based upon misinformation or lack of information.

Recognizing Ethnocentrism The ability to recognize attitudes or opinions that express the view that one's own race, culture, or group is inherently superior, or those attitudes that judge another culture or group in terms of one's own.

It is important to consider opposing viewpoints and equally important to be able to critically analyze those viewpoints. The activities in this book are designed to help the reader master these thinking skills. Statements are taken from the book's viewpoints and the reader is asked to analyze them. This technique aids the reader in developing skills that not only can be applied to the viewpoints in this book, but also to situations where opinionated spokespersons comment on controversial issues. Although the activities are helpful to the solitary reader, they are most useful when the reader can benefit from the interaction of group discussion.

Using this book and others in the series should help readers develop basic reading and thinking skills. These skills should improve the reader's ability to understand what they read. Readers should be better able to separate fact from opinion, substance from rhetoric and become better consumers of information in our media-centered culture.

This volume of the Opposing Viewpoints Series does not advocate a particular point of view. Quite the contrary! The very nature of the book leaves it to the reader to formulate the opinions he or she find most suitable. My purpose as publisher is to see that this is made possible by offering a wide range of viewpoints which are fairly presented.

David L. Bender
Publisher

Introduction

"America, in the assembly of nations, has uniformly spoken among them the language of equal liberty, equal justice and equal rights."

John Quincy Adams 1767-1848

The United States is just one of many countries born of the violence of revolution. Unlike many nations, however, the United States has consistently attempted to sustain the ideals chiseled from its revolutionary past. Justice, liberty, and equality remain American goals. Every schoolchild can recite Abraham Lincoln's moving words that bind equality inextricably with the goals of our nation: "Fourscore and seven years ago, our fathers brought forth on this continent a new nation, conceived in Liberty and dedicated to the proposition that all men are created equal." This idealism places America at the center of a basic dilemma: if equal justice is guaranteed all American citizens, how can Americans allow unequal conditions to exist?

In order to eradicate unequal conditions, the US government has played in the past, and continues to play, a substantial role. Social security, the New Deal, affirmative action, and the civil rights amendments are all examples of a government attempting to assure equal justice, the final aim being for America to exist both in reality, as in philosophy, as the country that places above all else the equality of all individuals.

However, government attempts to remove social inequities through regulation and legislation have often proven controversial. After all, it is argued, America is the land of opportunity and as such, individuals should be able to achieve their goals without the aid of government. In the middle of the 19th century, Horatio Alger's popular stories showed ordinary people succeeding in America simply by displaying industry and other allegedly positive personal qualities. Alger's "Match Stick" boy, Mark, rose above his humble beginnings by hard work, resolve, and cleverness. By becoming a self-made millionaire, Mark informed countless legions of American readers that success, acceptance, and equality could be achieved by personal, not governmental, initiative.

Not everyone agrees with Alger's optimism. Alexis de Tocqueville, for example believed inequality to be a natural state, one that people, government, and laws are unable to alter. In *Democracy in America* over a century ago he wrote: "People will never succeed in reducing all the conditions of society to a perfect level; and even if they unhappily attained that absolute and complete equality, inequality of minds would still remain." In contrast, Abraham Lincoln believed equality should be something "constantly looked to, constantly labored for and even though never perfectly attained, constantly approximated and thereby constantly spreading." He challenged America to strive toward the perfection of equality at all times.

Social Justice: Opposing Viewpoints makes clear that America's identity continues to be inextricably linked with the issue of equality. Four topics are debated: Is Affirmative Action Just? Are the Poor Treated Fairly? Are Immigrants Treated Fairly? and Do Women Recieve Equal Treatment? Each, while debating the problem of equality and justice in America, probes a deeply seated and underlying theme: What does America stand for? As readers explore these topics, they will find themselves embroiled in the themes that helped forge America's unique identity since its inception.

Is Affirmative Action Just?

"Affirmative action...rests on the conviction that the long-range goal of equal opportunity cannot be reached without color-sensitive and sex-sensitive policies in the present."

Affirmative Action Is Just

Wanda Warren Berry

Wanda Warren Berry is assistant professor of philosophy and religion and director of affirmative action at Colgate University in Hamilton, New York. She earned a B.A. from Boston University, a Master of Divinity from Yale, and a Ph.D. from Syracuse University. Dr. Berry describes herself as an interdisciplinarian in the humanities with a focus on religious studies and philosophy. She has authored numerous articles on those subjects. In the following viewpoint, Dr. Berry attacks one of the main criticisms of affirmative action, reverse discrimination. She argues that reverse discrimination should be the only goal of affirmative action, which should actively pursue the addition of minorities and women to the workforce.

As you read, consider the following questions:

1. What does Ms. Berry mean when she argues that affirmative action should not be race-neutral?
2. How does Ms. Berry use Plato's *Republic* to substantiate an argument against merit?
3. What is the "new heaven and earth" that Ms. Berry describes?

Wanda Warren Berry, "The Dialectics of Affirmative Action." Copyright 1983 Christian Century Foundation. Reprinted by permission from the November 30, 1983 issue of *The Christian Century*.

Debate over the validity of affirmative action as a strategy for redressing some of the systemic inequities of our society stirred again this past summer when the administration nominated to the Civil Rights Commission three people known to be negative toward the affirmative-action concept. President Reagan has *patriotism* defended his nominees as strong civil rights advocates; but he also warned: "They don't believe that you can remedy past discrimination by creating new discrimination." I suggest that this tendency to identify affirmative action as a form of "new" or "reverse" discrimination not only forgets the original meaning of affirmative action, it also ignores its compatibility with some of the most treasured philosophical and religious traditions in which our democracy is rooted....

Affirmative Action and Race

Those who claim that affirmative action must be "neutral" fail to understand the way in which it goes beyond nondiscrimination. The normative formulation of the meaning of "affirmative-action programs" is found in the regulations issued in 1971 by the Office of Federal Contract Compliance of the U.S. Department of Labor, which spell out the implications of Executive Order 11246 for federal contractors. When such employers had a history of underusing minorities and women, they were required to institute programs that went beyond passive nondiscrimination through deliberate efforts to identify people of "affected classes" for the sake of advancing their employment. Other employers who were not federal contractors, but who *voluntarily* adopted affirmative-action plans, bound themselves to the basic principles enunciated in this document. Many institutions of higher education developed their affirmative-action plans in terms of the 1972 guidelines issued by the Department of Health, Education and Welfare, which made it clear that Executive Order 11246 embodies two concepts: *"Nondiscrimination* requires the elimination of all existing discriminatory conditions, whether purposeful or inadvertent....*Affirmative action* requires...the employer to make additional efforts to recruit, employ and promote qualified members of groups formerly excluded."

This definition shows the kind of dialectical concept which is required if we are to avoid simplistic solutions. For the sake of *reason* future nondiscrimination, affirmative action advocates suggest "positive discrimination." It rests on the conviction that the long- *objective reason* range goal of equal opportunity cannot be reached without color-sensitive and sex-sensitive policies in the present. The strategy of identifying persons in terms of race and sex recognizes that *reason* human beings are *both* profoundly historical (i.e., determined by *2* the past) *and* able consciously to choose procedures which change history in the direction of intended values.

17

The categories now associated with affirmative action were developed in government documents which call upon employers to undergo a *"utilization analysis"* of their present work force in order to develop "specific and result-oriented *procedures*" to which the employer commits *"every good-faith effort"* in order to provide "relief for members of an *'affected class,'* who by virtue of *past discrimination* continue to suffer the present effects of that discrimination." The self-analysis is supposed to discover areas in which such affected classes are underused, considering their availablity and skills. *"Goals and timetables"* are to be developed to guide efforts to correct deficiencies in the employment of affected class people in each level and segment of the work force. Affirmative action also calls for "rigorous examination" of standards and criteria for job performance, not so as to "dilute necessary standards," but in order to ensure that "arbitrary and discriminatory employment practices are eliminated" and that there are no unnecessary criteria which "have had the effect of eliminating women and minorities" either from selection or promotion.

The premise of this affirmative-action apparatus seems to be the following: if fewer women and minorities are employed than are available, there are systemic discriminatory patterns, even when there are no recognizable individual acts of discrimination. Affirmative action also presupposes that such institutionalized racism or sexism will continue to work its effects unless there is both rigorous public scrutiny of all employment proceedings and vigorous effort to bring women and minorities into organizations so that attitudes are changed. Thus affirmative-action programs both recognize the power of all of those factors in human life which transcend conscious individual control (systems, institutions, habits, traditions, the unconscious, the tacit, the inadvertent, the irrational) and appeal to human ability to act consciously with "good-faith effort" to implement chosen values. These programs not only admit the real power of past history in shaping our present, they also insist on procedures (e.g., monitoring and reporting) which will continue to "watchdog" us even after we have consciously chosen the goal of diversifying the work force through seeking those previously excluded.

Although individuals may not appropriate the history of our society as their responsibility, affirmative action requires the government to do so, denying support to employers who do not participate in the communally chosen goal of deliberate action toward equalizing opportunity. Current impatience with affirmative action may well derive from the narcissism of the culture. Fewer and fewer people hold philosophical and religious convictions that make them feel responsible to do something about institutionalized prejudice....

Modern societies have had little patience with the aristocratic notion of the just society proposed by Plato's *Republic*, which relies on a relatively fixed economic class system. Nevertheless, they have continued to be inspired by its ideal of granting authority to *aristos*, "the best." This is the case especially in personal ethics and in educational systems, in which the dialectic between respect for excellence and for the populace (*demos*) has tended to favor *arete* (excellence or virtue). One could say that the traditional American values have been formed in the dialectic between democracy and excellence. Americans have tended to think that Plato contradicted his own best insight, that "every soul has the power to know the truth," when he assumed that democracy necessarily threatens excellence.

It is often assumed that affirmative action asks for a "lowering of standards," that it sacrifices excellence for the sake of equality. But rightly understood, affirmative action preserves the dialectic between democracy and excellence which has been characteristic of America. Present legislation does not mandate employing people unqualified for certain jobs. It does insist, however, that we avoid the kind of unnecessary escalation of criteria for selection and promotion which has sometimes been used to keep certain classes of people from entering the mainstream of our economic life—in which they might help us to develop new kinds of excellence. Thus the American Association of University Professors' 1982 statement on affirmative action quotes at the outset its own 1973 report on "Affirmative Action in Higher Education," saying,

What is sought in the idea of affirmative action is essentially the revision of standards and practices to assure that institutions are in fact drawing from the largest marketplace of human resources in staffing their faculties and a critical review of appointment and advancement criteria to insure that they do not inadvertently foreclose consideration of the best qualified persons by untested presuppositions which operate to exclude women and minorities.

Quotas Are Fair When They're Fair

We sometimes use inappropriate ways to measure merit. Shouldn't merit still be the basis for our choices? Theoretically, yes. Practically, it seldom is. For most of the coveted jobs there simply is no way to select a "best" applicant. You simply cannot say which patrolman will make the "best" sergeant on the Detroit police force; you cannot even say which existing sergeant is the best. It depends.

And one of the things that it depends on is its effect on the question of representation, the appearance of fairness. To take a personal example, I am a member of the Pulitzer Prize board, a group of 16 journalists, newspaper executives, and academicians. Was I chosen, at least in significant part, because I am black? Of course. So was Hanna Gray, president of the University of Chicago, named to the Pulitzer group in part because she is a woman. Sandra Day O'Connor and Thurgood Marshall sit on the U.S. Supreme Court in part because she is female and he is black.

Does that constitute discrimination against white males not chosen for these posts? Of course not. Does the appointment of these particular people, all of them demonstrably competent, accomplish something worthwhile? Yes. It is important that society's institutions (including its workplaces) reflect the society. Are the people thus selected the best-qualified of all those who might like to give?

The question simply can't be answered.

reason Talk of "revision of standards and practices" might threaten traditional meritocracies, but it in no way endangers the healthy growth of an excellent human being in community with others. It is notable that the AAUP (even after the Bakke decision) supports "race- or sex-sensitive" selectivity. The AAUP has held to its earlier position that the faculty of an institution can authorize race- and sex-sensitive selectivity out of its conviction that human diversity is necessary for its professional excellence and for the excellence of the institution in which it teaches.

relate Many critics of affirmative action worry about singling out particular classes of people by race and sex, rather than assuming neutrality in employment practices. For them justice is a universal moral law which ignores all particulars....

Forgiveness and Affirmative Action

Affirmative-action officers are often accused of "suspiciousness" as they scrutinize practices for both advertent and inadvertent unfairness. They maintain relationships and fight despair only by remembering the unconsciousness of so much prejudice. Nevertheless, forgiveness cannot be the dominant mode of affirmative action. Instead, affirmative action must always insist that we see ourselves in terms of free responsibility to pursue chosen purposes rather than passively yielding to a fatalistic sense of powerlessness. Our society has chosen affirmative action as an interim strategy to deal with intransigent evils for which we all must accept responsibility. Affirmative action advocates must "watchdog" equal-opportunity procedures and practices as well as press for the increased presence of women and minorities at all levels of our work force, so that there might someday be that "new heaven and earth" in which our unconsciousness has been transformed through the good will which affirmative action calls "good-faith effort."

When affirmative-action officers must spend so much time hearing grievances and scrutinizing institutions for both deliberate and inadvertent racism and sexism, they face the danger of becoming habituated only to what philosopher Paul Ricoeur has called the "hermeneutics of suspicion." Ricoeur credits Freud with the creation of our modern suspiciousness, which always looks for the underlying, unconscious determinants of every action. Affirmative action tends to proceed in terms of this modern psychological awareness of the power of inadvertent factors in human life; but it also appeals to conscious intentions "to lead a new life," at least to the extent of exerting "good-faith effort" toward institutionally established goals. The "hermeneutics of suspicion" must ever be challenged by the "hermeneutics of hope," which relies upon our created ability to choose community. Affirmative action affirms: Knowing the power of unconscious prejudice and the inertia of privilege, we must act in terms of our ability to change the world, step by nitty-gritty step.

"More discrimination is simply not the way to end discrimination."

Affirmative Action Is Unjust

William Bradford Reynolds

William Bradford Reynolds earned a B.A. from Yale and a J.D. from Vanderbilt University in Tennessee in 1967. He is the assistant attorney general in the civil rights division under the Reagan administration and remains a controversial figure because of his views on affirmative action. In the following viewpoint, excerpted from a speech given before the Washington Center Legal Symposium on January 4, 1984, Mr. Reynolds states his belief that affirmative action is unjust because the program calls for hiring on the basis of race instead of merit or qualifications.

As you read, consider the following questions:

1. According to Mr. Reynolds, how does the modern affirmative action plan differ from its original purpose?
2. Have civil rights leaders opposed or supported affirmative action, according to the author?
3. What does the author mean when he says affirmative action should be race-neutral?
4. Why does Mr. Reynolds believe that affirmative action violates our rights as individuals?

William Bradford Reynolds, in a speech before The Washington Center Legal Symposium, January 4, 1984.

"Affirmative action," as that term was originally used and understood in the early 1960's—indeed through the 1960's—carried with it no connotation or suggestion of preferential treatment. Rather, it was a term of art descriptive of affirmative recruitment and outreach efforts designed to embrace those who had previously been ignored, or purposefully excluded from consideration, and thus effectively denied any opportunity to participate as individuals in the competitive employment process. It is interesting for those of you who are statistically oriented that the utilization of "affirmative action" in this, its traditional sense, brought significant increases in the minority workforce of this country throughout the 1960's, increases that, regrettably, were not maintained for significant portions of the black population in the 1970's under a different regime of "affirmative action." But I am getting ahead of myself.

Race-Neutral Affirmative Action

Race-neutral "affirmative action"—and my discussion has equal application to the characteristics of gender, ethnic origin and religion—race-neutral "affirmative action" contravenes neither law nor public policy. But, when the term "affirmative action" takes on the definitional gloss provided in the 1970's—the gloss of racial goals, quotas or set-asides that, by design, prefer certain individuals over others solely because of skin color—not only law and policy, but also the moral values on which this great country was founded, are insufferably offended. For, what is invariably involved under such a regime of preferential treatment is discrimination, and no matter what the excuse or how elaborate the rationale, it remains irrefutably the case that: "no discrimination based on race is benign,...no action disadvantaging a person because of his [or her] color is affirmative."...

None was more passionately committed to the colorblind principle of equal opportunity for all than the leaders of the civil rights movement, who had for so many years courageously marched in bold defiance of those bent on ordering society according to the color of a person's skin. Preferential treatment based on race was, to them, intolerable, regardless of the purpose. Roy Wilkins, while he was Executive Director of the NAACP, stated the position unabashedly during congressional consideration of the 1964 civil rights laws. "Our association has never been in favor of a quota system," he testified. "We believe the quota system is unfair whether it is used for [blacks] or against [blacks]...[W]e feel people ought to be hired because of their ability, irrespective of their color....We want equality, equality of opportunity and employment on the basis of ability."...

It was during this era that the concept of "affirmative action" first gained prominence in a civil rights context, not—as I have indicated—as a race-conscious tool for repairing employment discrimination, but, consistent with the time, as a recruitment or outreach measure designed to operate in a race-neutral manner. This traditional understanding of affirmative action held sway through the 1960's.

But then the colorblind ideal that had been the civil rights rallying cry for over a decade began to give ground in the 1970's to a new demand. Instead of race neutrality, "racial balance" and "racial preference" were increasingly advanced as necessary means of overcoming racial discrimination. The quest for equal opportunity evolved, in many quarters, into an insistence upon equality of results.

Steve Kelley, *The San Diego Union*, reprinted with permission.

Those in the forefront of this movement embrace numerical parity, or at least numerical proportionality, as the test of non-discrimination. Regulation and allocation by race, they maintain, are not wrong *per se*. Rather, their validity depends upon who is being regulated, on what is being allocated and on the purpose of the arrangement. If a racial preference will achieve the desired statistical result, its discriminatory feature can be tolerated, we are told, as an unfortunate but necessary consequence of remedying the effects of past discrimination—using race "in order to get beyond racism" is the way one member of the Supreme Court put it. Thus, Justice Jackson's prophetic warning in *Korematsu* almost 40 years ago can no longer be so lightly dismissed: an urgent need has been pressed and those intent on finding a quick response, rather than a lasting solution, have reached for the loaded weapon—the so-called remedial, or benign, use of racial discrimination.

Preferred Race Only Temporary

Apparently, we are to take some comfort in the promise that the disadvantage to those who are not members of the preferred racial class will be only temporary. Once the effects of past discrimination are eliminated, we are assured, society can again turn to equal opportunity as its guiding principle.

The unanswered question, of course, is "how temporary is temporary?" We are told that our tolerance of race preferences need last only until the effects of past discrimination are removed. But, how are we to know when that day arrives? And, by what mystical process are we then to convert to a policy of race neutrality?

Even more fundamentally, can it realistically be maintained that either numerical parity or proportional representation is any measure of success? In an environment totally free from unlawful discrimination, participation in any given endeavor will inevitably be the product of individual interest, industry, talent and merit. As Morris Abram observed in testifying before the Senate Subcommittee on the Constitution, job applicants simply "do not come proportionately qualified by race, gender and ethnic origin in accordance with U.S. population statistics." Nor do the career interests of individuals break down proportionately among racial groups. Indeed, is there any human endeavor, since the beginning of time, that has attracted persons sharing a common physical characteristic in numbers proportional to the representation of such persons in the community?

Past Discrimination Redressed

What sense, then, does it make to seek to redress "the effects of past discrimination" in such a fashion? We live in a pluralistic society in which numerous groups compete for the limited economic and educational resources available. To prefer one over another "temporarily" in order to achieve racial proportionality requires a similar allocation to every other discrete racial, ethnic or religious group that can sustain a claim of underrepresentation. Are we really prepared to assign Government the role of dispenser of life's benefits, giving here, taking away there—all without regard to individual merit—until, presumably, all preferred classes are in equipoise? And, if so, does there realistically

25

ever come a time when the guiding hand that somehow strikes the perfect balance can be removed and we return again to the ideal of equal opportunity? I fear not.

It is, therefore, for me, far more faithful to the objective of eliminating the effects of past discrimination to emphasize individual relief and nondiscrimination rather than group representation and further discrimination. Can it reasonably be maintained that those who were subjected in the past to the indignity of prejudgment based on their race are benefitted today by a remedy which ensures that their children and grandchildren will continue to be prejudged and allocated opportunity based on race? Does the person selected by reason of a racial classification suffer any less indignity than the person excluded?

Minority Success and Affirmative Action

I'm against quotas, proportional representation or the setting aside of government contracts for minority businesses.

In many cases, affirmative action takes away from legitimate minority success. People look at the black banker downtown who has made it on his own and say, "He got his job because of affirmative action." Or, an employer hires a few talented minority people who would have succeeded anyway and says, "Those are my affirmative-action hires."

Clarence M. Pendleton Jr., "A Reaganite View of Civil Rights Today," *U.S. News & World Report*, September 27, 1982.

Let me offer the response of Professor Alexander Bickel in his classic book, *The Morality of Consent*: "The history of the racial quota is a history of subjugation, not beneficence....[T]he quota is a divider of society, a creator of castes, and it is all the worse for its racial base, especially in a society desperately striving for an equality that will make race irrelevant." Justice William O. Douglas made the same point in constitutional terms, stating: "The Equal Protection Clause commands the elimination of racial barriers, not their creation in order to satisfy our theory as to how society ought to be organized...."

Quotas Erect Barriers

That, of course, is precisely what quotas (or any other race-based numerical preference) do: they erect artificial barriers that let some in and keep others out, not on the basis of ability, but on the basis of the most irrelevant of characteristics under law—race. They turn upside down the dream of Dr. Martin Luther King, Jr.—the dream that some day society will judge people "not by the color of their skin, but by the content of their character."

Perhaps the cruelest irony is that, in the broadest sense, color-conscious measures pose the greatest threat to members of minority groups because it is they who are, by definition, outnumbered. In the narrower sense, members of all racial groups stand to suffer, because an individual's energy, ability, enthusiasm, imagination and effort can take him no farther than permitted by his group's allotment or quota. What has long been a pursuit of equality of opportunity is thus in danger of becoming a forfeiture of opportunity in absolute terms: *individual* opportunity is being sacrificed at the expense of *group-oriented* ambitions, measured in terms of proportional representation and proportional results. And this is in spite of the fact that, as Justice Powell observed in his controlling opinion in *Bakke*, "[n]othing in the Constitution supports the notion that individuals may be asked to suffer otherwise impermissible burdens in order to enhance the societal standing of their ethnic groups."

Government Polarizes Races

The more insistent Government is on the use of racial preferences—whether in the form of quotas, goals or any other numerical device—to correct what is perceived as an "imbalance" in our schools, our neighborhoods, our work places, or our elected bodies, the more racially polarized society becomes. Such a selection process encourages us to stereotype our fellow human beings—to view their advancements, not as hard-won achievements, but as conferred benefits. It invites us to look upon people as possessors of racial characteristics, not as the unique individuals they are. It breeds nagging self-doubts with respect to one's own accomplishments. In a word, it submerges the vitality of personality under the deadening prejudgments of race.

The very purpose intended to be served is defeated, for race-based preferences cut against the grain of equal opportunity. And, while we are told that this is but an interim condition in the interest of achieving "equal results," let us not forget that it was the same justification (*i.e.,* achieving "equal results") that sustained for over a half a century the separate-but-equal doctrine—which likewise looked to membership in a particular racial group as an accepted basis for according individuals different treatment.

Using Alcohol to Treat Alcoholism

That stark reality provides a ready answer to those who argue that we must use race "to get beyond racism." What nonsense! Would anyone seriously prescribe the use of alcohol to get beyond alcoholism? History teaches all too well that a race-conscious approach does not work. It is wrong when operated by government to bestow advantages on whites at the expense of innocent blacks; it assumes no greater claim of morality if "the tables are turned." More discrimination is simply not the way to end

27

discrimination.

Our rights in this country derive from the uniquely American belief in the primacy of the individual. And in no instance should an individual's rights rise any higher or fall any lower than the rights of others because of race, gender or ethnic origin. Whatever group membership one inherits, it carries with it no entitlement to preferential treatment over those not similarly endowed with the same immutable characteristics. Any compromise of this principle is discrimination, plain and simple, and such behavior is no more tolerable when employed remedially, in the name of "affirmative action," to bestow a gratuitous advantage on members of a particular group, than when it is divorced from such beneficence and for the most invidious of reasons works to one's disadvantage.

The Constitution and Affirmative Action

Doesn't preferential treatment for minorities violate the Constitution and/or the Civil Rights Act? Well, hardly, as it turns out.

Justice Powell, the man who wrote so passionately about the Constitution protecting individuals and not groups in the Bakke case, made two exceptions to his anathema on groupthink. First, race can be considered "as a factor" among others in an admissions (or, presumable hiring) decision. Second, *any* form of reverse discrimination—even explicit quotas—is permissible as a "remedy," following an official judicial, legislative or executive finding of past discrimination. In other words, the Constitution forbids you to engage in reverse discrimination by yourself, but requires you to do it when ordered to by someone else, like a judge.

Michael Kinsley, "Equal Lack of Opportunity," *Harper's*, June 1983.

It is for this reason that I believe—and believe very strongly— that there is but one course to steer if we are to eliminate the cancer of race discrimination from the body politic once and for all. As recognized by Justice William O. Douglas, by Senator Hubert H. Humphrey, by Professor Alexander Bickel, by Roy Wilkins, and by the framers of the 1964 civil rights laws and the Fourteenth Amendment, the most direct route to a color-blind society is along the path of race-neutrality. Professor William Van Alstyne put it best, I think, in his Chicago Law Review article, "Rites of Passages: Race, the Supreme Court, and the Constitution":

...one gets beyond racism by getting beyond it now: by a complete, resolute, and credible commitment *never* to tolerate in one's own life—or in the life or practices of one's government—the differential treatment of other human beings by race. Indeed, that is the great lesson for government itself to teach; in all we do in life, whatever we do in life, to treat any person less well than another or to favor any more than another for being black or white or brown or red, is wrong. Let that be our fundamental law and we shall have a Constitution universally worth expounding.

If we follow that sound advice, the evil of discrimination that has plagued us for so many years can soon begin to be discussed largely as a problem of the past, rather than a "brooding omnipresence" that continues to haunt us for the future. If we do not, but rather continue to pursue group-oriented, color-conscious solutions, my prediction is that—as benign as the intent may be—we will advance no closer to a realization of the dream of Dr. Martin Luther King, Jr., and, indeed, could well find ourselves in 1996 in a racially-ordered society similar to that approved by the *Plessy* Court in 1896.

"Preferential policies should be supported by anyone committed to eradicating gross economic injustice."

Affirmative Action Compensates for Past Discrimination

Diana Axelson

Diana Axelson is associate professor and chairperson of the Department of Philosophy of Spelman College in Atlanta, Georgia. She received her degrees from Stanford University and is the author of numerous articles on ethical issues in human experimentation and on the care of handicapped newborns. In the following viewpoint, Ms. Axelson discusses her belief that minorities should be compensated for the discriminatory treatment they and their ancestors received in the past.

As you read consider the following questions:

1. What are the three values Ms. Axelson believes justify affirmative action?
2. What are the three types of compensation to which Ms. Axelson refers?
3. What four objections to compensation does the author discount?

Copyright 1978 by Philosophical Forum. First published in *Philosophical Forum* 9 (1978): 264-268. Reprinted by permission.

One of the issues which has most blatantly revealed the racist and sexist nature of American institutions is the implementation of affirmative action programs and stronger preferential policies in education and employment. The most striking characteristic of many discussions of such policies is the absence of any serious historical perspective on the role that genocide and cultural imperialism have played in the development of this country, and, in particular, in the evolution of its patterns of distribution of economic, political, and social power. In this article I shall summarize some of the main values relevant to the issue of preferential policies; examine some of the criticisms raised against such policies; consider some of the arguments which support them; and, finally, argue that an important justification for preferential policies can be based on the right of individuals and groups to reparations for past and present injustices....

An Outline of Relevant Values

The first step in understanding the problem is to identify the relevant ethical values. There seem to be at least three:

1. The obligation to pursue policies that meet the criteria of distributive justice, and, in particular, the obligation not to discriminate on morally irrelevant grounds in distributing social benefits such as jobs and educational places. We shall assume that distributive justice requires us to provide equality of opportunity, and thus in some cases to provide compensation for handicaps which prevent persons from competing on an equal basis for social benefits. Thus, for example, providing special training for blind persons could be seen as a form of compensation falling within the range of distributive justice. The ways in which such needs arise may be quite varied, and an adequate system of distributive justice will presumably provide for the contingencies identified by rational persons.

2. The obligation to promote social welfare, e.g., by ensuring a distribution of skills that is relatively efficient yet preserves other values the society may stress, such as some degree of freedom of choice in work roles.

3. The obligations of compensatory justice, to compensate victims of injustice. Here we are using the concept of compensatory justice to refer to one's right to remedy for some injury he or she has suffered in violation of his or her rights. In this sense, one is entitled to such benefits only when a prior injustice has occurred....

Obligations of Distributive Justice

The concepts of equality and non-discrimination are central in our discussion. A discriminatory practice or policy is typically taken to be one which makes unjust distinctions among persons.

Thus, definition of a discriminatory policy in employment or education presupposes a general concept of distributive justice as applied to social policy....

The demands of distributive justice, as we shall see, provide prominent arguments for opposing preferential policies or "reverse discrimination." Inequalities based simply on race or sex do not typically benefit all who participate in the practice, although they may do so in specific cases to be discussed below. Often, in the course of righting earlier wrongs, injustice may be done to others, specifically, to white males....

We must decide whether our aim is to maintain, reform, or destroy existing practices and the larger social institutions surrounding them. A revolutionary might see favoring minorities and women as morally unjustifiable because it fosters acceptance of the economic and social systems within which unjust practices exist....

The Reality of Minority Discrimination

The [Reagan] Administration will have nothing to do with class actions in employment discrimination cases. It spent more than a year opposing a voting rights bill designed to allow general relief from discriminatory voting practices.

The Administration's underlying rationale is that the Constitution is "color-blind," and does not protect classes or categories of minorities unless each member can prove individually that he or she was a victim of intentional discrimination. In addition to being burdensome and unrealistic, this approach to civil rights enforcement is fundamentally at odds with the development of remedies responding to the history of race and sex discrimination in the United States. Can anyone doubt in 1982 that minorities and women as classes have been and are being discriminated against? The Administration's "color-blind" civil rights policy is blind to the reality of illegal discrimination and the efforts of the last three decades to address that reality."

John Shattuck, in a speech delivered at the American Bar Association's annual convention in August 1982.

However, this objection seems to overlook the realities of racism in the U.S. today, as it is expressed in the economic and legal systems. Using 1970 statistics from the U.S. Census Bureau, Victor Perlo has documented the radical economic inequalities in the U.S. and shown that the most striking correlations are between poverty and race.....He argues,

The ending of discrimination requires concretely defined preferential treatment of Blacks in admission, employment, etc. Minimum numbers and percentages of Blacks and maximum time limits must be specified. Machinery for systematic checkup and penalties must be provided, sufficiently severe to deter noncompliance.

Perlo also points out the relatively minor effect of such measures on whites:

> ...an increase in Black admissions to law school from 5% to 15%—using hypothetical figures—represents an increase of 200%, while the corresponding reduction in the admission of whites, from 95% to 85% of the total, represents a decline of only a little more than 10%....the decline in percentage of admissions according to whites will not be in any sense discrimination against whites, but merely the correction of historical discrimination in favor of whites.

Perlo concludes that preferential policies should be supported by anyone committed to eradicating gross economic injustice, whether one favors the continuance of capitalism or regards socialism as necessary for the achievement of full human equality.

Obligations of Compensatory Justice

One of the most powerful arguments for preferential policies rests on the moral claims of ethnic minorities and women for compensation....

The first form of compensation which seems appropriate is compensation to persons now living, for injuries they themselves have received as a result of individualized or institutionalized racism and sexism. One could include here the psychological effects of sexual and racial stereotypes in the mass media, as well as the effects of more clearly defined institutions such as the Federal government, the public schools, and the judicial system. Note that we refer here to injuries to the persons who shall receive compensation, not to injuries received by their ancestors. Neither this form of compensation nor the following one requires an appeal to the principle that persons now living are entitled to compensation simply in virtue of their blood relationships to persons injured at an earlier time.

The second form of compensation which seems appropriate is compensation to persons now living, for present inequities resulting from earlier injustices. The claim here is that many people in the United States—primarily whites—have privileges which are unjust because they derive from prior exploitation of ethnic minorities. Arnold Kaufman formulated this principle as it applies to Blacks and whites in the U.S., as follows:

> The sons of privilege are being asked to compensate the sons of slaves whether or not the former are responsible for the disabilities of the latter....It is not claimed that the sons of slavemasters are sinners because their fathers sinned. Rather, the demand that the sons of slavemasters make restitution to the sons of slaves rests on the claim that the former enjoy great and undeserved advantages, as a result of accidents of social inheritance directly connected to the existence of slavery.

Thus demands for compensation from living whites are based on their possession of undeserved benefits, not on the basis of specific actions. The principle could be extended to claims by other groups suffering similar inequities deriving from exploitation. The existence of rights of inheritance in the U.S. is one basis for these claims, though formal inheritance is by no means the only way by which economic and political powers have been transmitted....

While many ethnic groups in the United States have been victims of discrimination, past and present genocidal actions have been directed toward some groups on a scale so massive that it is difficult to imagine any adequate reparation. The extermination or near-extermination of various Native American peoples; the experience of slavery and the racism which continues today; and the annexation of portions of Mexico and the subsequent policies towards Mexicans and Mexican-Americans are examples of the sort of oppression which makes compensation a moral imperative. In identifying groups entitled to compensation, it is important to be sensitive to disrespect for life, economic exploitation, and political disenfranchisement. The existence of cultural imperialism is also an important part of the record. Current statistics on social welfare are also relevant, since they help to identify groups which benefit least from American wealth. Among the most significant statistics are those relating to life expectancy, infant mortality rates, family income, unemployment rates, job status, and levels of educational attainment. Examination of such statistics, and their underlying causes, bears out the claim that discriminatory practices of the past continue to have concrete manifestations today....

Objections to Preferential Policies

In this paper I shall not argue extensively for what I take to be the obvious fact that certain ethnic minorities, and men generally, have suffered injuries and inequities....

A variety of objections to preferential policies are frequently raised. We shall examine four of these.

1. *Failure to fit the ideal model of compensation*

In following preferential policies in employment and education, it seems highly impractical to consider each person's case individually. Thus, if reparations are directed toward groups, it is possible that they may sometimes be made to individuals who do not deserve compensation, or at least to those who are not as deserving as a white male who has suffered discrimination....

2. *The dangers of the quota system*

Another objection to preferential policies, when accompanied by specific time tables and quota systems, is that such procedures will threaten the maintenance of distributive justice.

3. *The problem of "where to stop"*

A similar concern is voiced by persons who feel that demands for reparations cannot be given in appropriate quantitative terms. This problem is seen as raising the danger of giving too much in the way of reparations, and thus of creating a new injustice.

To Judge on Merit or Race?

Opponents of affirmative action are hung up on a distinction that seems more profoundly irrelevant: treating individuals versus treating groups. What is the moral difference between dispensing favors to people on their "merits" as individuals and passing out society's benefits on the basis of group identification?

Group identifications like race and sex are, of course, immutable. They have nothing to do with a person's moral worth. But the same is true of most of what comes under the label "merit." The tools you need for getting ahead in a meritocratic society—not all of them but most: talent, education, instilled cultural values such as ambition—are distributed just as arbitrarily as skin color. They are fate. The notion that people somehow "deserve" the advantages of these characteristics in a way they don't "deserve" the advantages of their race is powerful, but illogical.

Michael Kinsley, "Equal Lack of Opportunity," *Harper's,* June 1983.

4. *The irrelevance of historical analysis*

Finally, there are those who would resist the appeal to historical analysis as a basis for distinguishing among ethnic groups. The western response, reflecting a patriarchal white male interpretation of experience, tends to see such historical perspectives as appeals to a principle of vengeance. While acknowledging that current discrimination should be abolished, and that injuries done to those now living deserve compensation, the notion of reparations due as a result of psychological alliance with one's foreparents is seen as indefensible.

Reasons for Preferential Policies

1. *Transition to a just state*

There are several ways of responding to these criticisms. First, one can argue that preferential policies will hasten progress toward distributive justice in relatively straightforward ways. Such policies can be expected to produce desirable psychological changes among ethnic minorities and women. For example, members of these groups are likely to develop new aspirations as a result of having role models in positions where there are now few such persons. Second, favoring minorities and women in jobs and education will lead to a more nearly just distribution of economic and legal representation. Such a redistribution is not only desirable in itself but also will make possible further redistribution in the directions of social justice.

2. *The issue of merit*

Secondly, preferential policies force us to take a serious look at the entire concept of merit. The question of merit raises at least three different issues:

a. Deciding what constitutes appropriate criteria of merit;

b. Deciding whether a given applicant meets these criteria, and perhaps to what degree he or she does so; and,

c. Ensuring that the chosen criteria are in fact used as a basis for selection.

Minority members and women have charged that none of these tasks is presently adequately carried out in all areas of employment and education. Criticism on this point has come from diverse sources. For example, economist Milton Friedman has emphasized the difficulty of setting and enforcing meaningful standards for employment. While his aim is to argue against governmental intervention in employment, his criticism of licensing procedures is relevant to the problem of merit. Though such procedures are supposed to impose standards of performance in various areas, he claims that:

> ...any relationship between the requirements imposed and the qualities which the licensure is intended to assure is rather far-fetched. The extent to which such requirements go is sometimes little short of ludicrous.

The areas of licensing and testing for merit really point to the underlying problem of interest groups which use these supposed criteria of merit to maintain their own power....

Groups of Victims Overlap

3. *Overlap of groups victimized by discrimination*

One other consideration should be noted before we move in more detail to the reparations issue. There is a notable overlap of certain ethnic minorities with other groups which have been discriminated against: e.g., disproportionately large numbers of Blacks, Chicanos, and Native Americans are poor and have arrest records....

While our discussion here is confined to discrimination within the area of employment, the correlation between being non-white and having an arrest record or a history of drug usage points to much broader issues of social justice. To explore these would reinforce the legitimacy of minority claims for reparations.

4. *Magnitude of reparations due and improbability of adequate reparation*

Even if one acknowledges that some inequities will result if such policies are followed, one can still argue that still greater inequities will result if such policies are not followed....

I believe that until adequate reparations are made to ethnic minorities and women, there will continue to be justifiable resentment on the part of those members of these groups who see themselves as psychologically allied to their foreparents. To claim that such resentment—hardly a pleasant state—constitutes a basis for reparations is not simply to appeal to a principle of vengeance. It is to appeal to a violation of one of the rights guaranteed by distributive justice, namely, the right to recognition of one's worth and dignity as a person. The sense of identification involved in such a violation cannot be adequately understood within an individualistic world-view. If one's concept of self-identity includes the being of one's ancestors, then one does not suffer simply on behalf of one's ancestors; rather, the suffering is one's own. Moreover, the identification does not arise only out of anger. It reflects, too, the positive sense of community which many of us feel with some who have died, and the concern we feel for children in future generations. The interpretation of this attitude as an individualistic desire for revenge is a distortion of the love and communal interpretation of experience which motivates many of us to continue to struggle toward a just society....

Only when we move beyond the process of justifying minor measures such as preferential policies, and begin to confront realistically a massive restructuring of the social order, can we claim to be moving with any deliberate speed toward a genuinely just state. We must give those deserving reparations the tools to deal with these problems, rather than avoiding the moral issues by further debate about the moral or legal acceptability of reparations to the victims of American exploitation.

> *"It is impossible to rectify the consequences of all past wrongs."*

Affirmative Action Cannot Compensate for Past Discrimination

Michael Levin

Michael Levin is professor of philosophy at City College of New York and contributes articles to *Commentary* magazine. He is the author of *Metaphysics and the Mind-Body Problem* and of numerous papers on the foundation of logic and mathematics. In the following viewpoint, Mr. Levin explains why he believes that the goal of affirmative action is both immoral and irrational because it cannot be fulfilled.

As you read, consider the following questions:

1. Why are arguments that racial discrimination deserves special treatment invalid, according to Mr. Levin?
2. Why does Mr. Levin argue that patterned wrongs, like lynching, do not deserve special attention?
3. Why is compensation irrational, according to the author?

"Is Racial Discrimination Special?" by Michael Levin is reprinted from *Policy Review*, Fall 1982. *Policy Review* is a publication of The Heritage Foundation, 214 Massachusetts Avenue NE, Washington, DC 20002.

"Reverse discrimination" is the policy of favoring members of certain groups (usually racial), in situations in which merit has been at least ideally the criterion, on the grounds that *past* members of these groups have suffered discrimination. Giving someone a job he was denied because *he* was discriminated against does not come under this heading, since such redress is justified by ordinary canons of justice, in particular that of giving someone what he is owed. I am referring, rather, to the practice of hiring or admitting a preset number of (e.g.) blacks regardless of whether the blacks so hired have been wronged, and regardless of the qualifications of competing whites. The difference between the two policies is the difference between restoring a robbery victim's property to him, and hunting up the descendants of robbery victims and giving them goods at the expense of people who robbed no one. I have no quarrel with the former, many quarrels with the latter: reverse discrimination is as ill-advised a course of action as any undertaken by this country in at least a century. It cannot be justified by its social benefits, since experience suggests that this policy is proving disastrous. It cannot be justified as giving particular members of the chosen group what they would have gotten if they had not been discriminated against, since by stipulation "affirmative action" (bureaucratese for reverse discrimination) goes beyond such an appeal to ordinary ideas of justice and compensation. It penalizes a group of present-day whites—those who are at least as well qualified but passed over—without proof that they have discriminated or directly benefitted from discrimination: whites no more responsible for past discrimination than anyone else. Lately, as the harmfulness and unfairness of reverse discrimination have become more evident, its proponents have taken to arguing that reverse discrimination is needed to prevent future discrimination. Such "preventive discrimination" has all the disadvantages of preventive detention and none of the advantages, such as the elimination of clear and present danger to life and limb.

Racial Discrimination Not Special

But such frontal assaults on reverse discrimination usually accomplish nothing, so I will not attempt one here. I will instead focus on a clear-cut issue which is central to the debate but which has, surprisingly, been almost completely ignored. It is this: what is so special about racial discrimination? Let me put the question more exactly. I will be arguing shortly that the only possible defense of reverse discrimination represents it as an attempt to rectify the consequences of past racial discrimination. But why has society selected one kind of wrong—discrimination—as particularly deserving or demanding rectification? Other past wrongs have left their traces—acts of theft, despoliation, fraud, anti-

39

Semitism—yet society has no organized policy of rectifying those wrongs. It surely seems that if the consequences of one kind of wrong should not be allowed to unfold, neither should those of any other. And this is what I want to establish: acts of racial discrimination have no morally special status. Important consequences flow from this. For reasons I will propose, it is fairly clear that society—in particular the employer—has no general standing obligation to block the consequences of past wrongs. So if discriminatory acts are no more deserving of rectification than wrong acts generally, no one is under any obligation at all to rectify them, or to be deprived so that these acts may be rectified.

Considering Race In Hiring

To request that we set and state numerical "goals" for hiring is to ask us to anticipate hiring on the basis of such "goals." It asks us to consider race or sex or color as reasonable ingredients in such decisions. But they are not. We would find it difficult to envision a time when the answer, "Because she was a black female," or, "Because he was a Jew," would be the legitimate response to the question, "Why did you hire or promote or fire this person?"

William Bennet, in response to a letter by Clarence Thomas insisting that the Endowment for the Humanities comply with federal quota guidelines.

With these preliminary points as background, let us look at the issue again. I noted that reverse discrimination discriminates against whites in a way that cannot be justified by ordinary notions of justice. Thus, if it is justifiable at all, it must be because we owe something to present-day blacks in some extraordinary sense. And the standard reason offered for saying that we do is that the blacks to be hired today bear the burdens of past discrimination. Had there been no racial discrimination, they would have been able to get those jobs; their qualifications would have been as good as those of the better-qualified whites they are displacing. It is sometimes added that all whites benefit in some way from past discrimination, so all whites owe blacks something, namely a more advantageous position. Affirmative action is supposed to rectify the consequences of past discrimination, to draw the sting from acts so bad that their consequences cannot be permitted to unfold....

Whatever we call it, the aim of affirmative action is to undo the consequences of past discrimination. But then the issue I raised becomes pressing. If there is nothing morally special about discrimination, nothing which makes it especially deserving of rectification, any policy that treats discrimination as if it were morally special is arbitrary and irrational....

Let me start with a truism. Discrimination deserves to be halted where it exists, and redressed where it can be, because it is *wrong*. Discrimination is worth doing something about because *wrongs* are worth doing something about and discrimination is wrong. Once we grant this, we start to see that there is nothing *sui generis* about discrimination. It competes with other wrongs for righting. And I take it as obvious that some wrongs demand righting more urgently than others.... So: denying a man a job on grounds of color is evidently just one among many ways of wronging him. It is far less egregious than assault or murder.

It is frequently but mistakenly claimed that racial discrimination is special because it involves a group. Certainly, an act of racial discrimination involves a whole group in the sense that it involves treating an individual not in his own right but insofar as he belongs to a group. But racial discrimination is not the only kind of act that is thus group-related. Many wrongs having nothing to do with race are discriminatory in the precise sense that they base the treatment of an individual on membership in a morally irrelevant group. Nepotism is discrimination against nonrelatives. When I make my lazy nephew district manager, I am disqualifying more able competitors because they belong to a group—non-family—membership in which should not count in the matter at hand. Discrimination need not be racial: any time you make a moral distinction on morally irrelevant grounds, you discriminate invidiously. In a society in which racial discrimination was unknown but capricious nepotism common, denial of due process on grounds of family would provoke as much indignation as racial discrimination does now.

It is sheer confusion to argue that acts of racial discrimination are special because they insult a whole race as well as wrong an individual. When I assault you, I assault no one else—and when I discriminate against you, I discriminate against no one else. True, my discrimination may indicate a readiness to discriminate against others and may create widespread anxiety—but my assaulting you may indicate a readiness to assault others and create even greater general anxiety....

Special Treatment for Blacks

Why are we willing to contemplate special treatment for blacks now, when we would not contemplate special treatment for someone whose ancestors were defrauded by a man who left no descendants? Because, I suspect, we think that by benefitting today's black we apologize for the long-ago insult to the race, and that this apology and benefit will somehow be transmitted back to the blacks who endured the original discrimination. Were this picture accurate, it might justify supposing that past discriminatory acts cast longer shadows than other wrongs. But it is just a myth.

41

A racial grouping no more deserves reification than does the class of people whose ancestors were defrauded. We resist the impulse to reify in the latter case only because the trait in question is not visually salient and has no especially coherent history....

Murder Victims and Special Treatment

Granted, racial wrongs have gone beyond discrimination in hiring or the use of public facilities, extending all the way to lynching. But to acknowledge this is to bring racial wrongs under independent headings—denial of due process, assault, murder. Lynching Emmet Till was wrong not because Emmet Till was black, but because lynching is murder. So if blacks deserve special treatment because of (say) this country's history of lynching, it is because descendants of murder victims deserve special treatment. But this concedes my point: what was wrong about especially egregious acts of racial discrimination is what is wrong about parallel nonracial acts; if we treat the former as special, we must treat the latter as special as well....

Government Control of Institutions

Here is the crux of the argument about quotas. If these preferences in reverse discrimination arise from aspirations only and not as a matter of right, then the imposition of quotas, goals, and timetables by government on private institutions represents an assertion of state power with major implications, implications which I believe should be resisted. Does a research university violate one's rights when it insists that language instructors have Ph.D. degrees, thus failing to attain some numerical proportion of minority teachers in its Romance language department?...If this criteria is not used by employers for the purpose of excluding members of minority groups, then to demand that employers override their own sense of how to run their institutions in order that they attain a fixed racial proportion is to assert a general power in the state to draft the private sector in pursuit of state's goals.

Charles Fried, "Questioning Quotas," *The New Republic*, December 26, 1983.

A subsidiary point. I have so far let pass one peculiarity of affirmative action programs: they award jobs or placement to rectify past wrongs. Yet normally when we compensate someone for wrongful deprivation, we give him the equivalent of what he lost, giving him the thing itself only when feasible. If your negligence costs a pianist his hands, you are not obliged to hire him to give a concert. The whole thrust of his complaint, after all, is that he is no longer competent to undertake such an enterprise. You owe him the money he could have made from concertizing, plus some monetary equivalent of the satisfaction he has lost through your negligence....

42

It is obvious that no employer has a general obligation to rectify wrongful acts, to offer extraordinary compensation. I am not speaking, again, of righting wrongs he perpetrates or directly benefits from. I mean that if, as a result of one wrong once done—not necessarily to an ancestor—I am worse off than I would have been; you, an arbitrarily chosen employer, have no obligation whatever to neutralize the consequences of that wrong. No one has any obligation to make me as well off as I would have been had that wrong not been committed. Why? Basically because it is *impossible* to rectify the consequences of all past wrongs. Consider how we might decide on compensatory payments....

What about limiting ourselves to rectifying wrongs we know about? But then we should surely try, indeed try as hard as possible, to find out about other wrongs, to trace their consequences, and rectify them. Once again, if we set out on that path, we will find ourselves with obligations that cannot be discharged. And an unmeetable obligation is no obligation at all. Indeed, it is far from obvious that the consequences of discrimination are easier to trace than those of other wrongs. I know victims of theft who have nothing to show for it. Why not benefit them? It is clearer that they are worse off from a past wrong than that an arbitrarily chosen black is....

Since, then, no one has any general rectificatory obligation, and since—as I argued earlier—past discrimination does not stand out from other wrongs as especially demanding rectification, I can see no justification at all for reverse discrimination.

I have embedded my main point in a somewhat complex context. Let me end by highlighting it. While racial discrimination is wrong, it is only one wrong among many and has no special claim on our moral attention. Past discrimination no more deserves extraordinary compensation than many other wrongs. And so any employment policy which does treat racial discrimination as special is arbitrary and irrational.

43

"Even during the best of times, there will be no change in the relative position of minorities unless affirmative action or other special measures are taken."

Affirmative Action Is Economically Necessary

Bernard E. Anderson

Bernard E. Anderson, economist, is director of the Social Sciences Division of the Rockefeller Foundation and president of the National Economic Association. In 1978-79, he was a member of the President's Commission on Unemployment Statistics. His publications include the books *Negro Employment in Public Utilities, Youth Employment: Public Policy,* and *Black Managers in American Business.* In the following viewpoint, Mr. Anderson states that the economic advancement of minorities can be directly tied to the success of affirmative action.

As you read, consider the following questions.

1. What statistics does Mr. Anderson cite to substantiate his view that affirmative action policies are still needed?
2. To what can the economic inequality between blacks and whites be attributed, according to Mr. Anderson?
3. Why does Mr. Anderson feel that AT&T is a good example of affirmative action working?

Bernard E. Anderson, "An Economic Defense of Affirmative Action," *Black Enterprise.*
Copyright May 1982, The Earl G. Graves Publishing Co. Inc., 130 Fifth Avenue, New York, NY 10011. All rights reserved.

Is affirmative action still necessary? Many critics argue that attitudes toward race relations have improved to a substantial degree and that discrimination is no longer a major factor in explaining employment and earnings disparities among minorities and others. According to these critics, economic growth and the expansion of jobs through unregulated, free market processes is all that is required to improve the economic status of minorities.

However, the available evidence suggests that just the reverse is true. Much of the progress achieved by minorities and women in some occupations and industries was either the direct result of or was substantially influenced by affirmative action remedies to employment discrimination.

Affirmative Action Is Necessary

The position of blacks and other minorities in the economy is like that of the caboose on a train. When the train speeds up, the caboose moves faster; when the train slows down, so does the caboose. No matter how fast the train goes, the caboose will never catch up with the engine unless special arrangements are made to change its position. So it is with minorities and the economy: Even during the best of times, there will be no change in the relative position of minorities unless affirmative action or other special measures are taken.

Policies designed to improve the relative position of minorities are justified by the continuing evidence of racial inequality in American economic life. In 1980, black unemployment was more than twice that of whites (13.2 percent vs. 6.3 percent). Unemployment among black teenagers, now officially reported at close to 50 percent, has been greater than 30 percent throughout the past decade, but has not reached that level among white youths in any year. Further, the employment/population ratio—for some purposes a more instructive measure of labor market participation than the unemployment rate—has steadily declined among black youths while increasing among whites. About 25 out of every 100 black youths had jobs in 1980, compared with 50 of every 100 whites.

Comparative income data also show continuing evidence of economic disparty between blacks and others. In 1979, the average black family had only $57 for every $100 enjoyed by whites. Even in families headed by persons fortunate enough to work year round, blacks have failed to achieve parity, earning only 77 percent of the income of comparable white families.

Effects of Past Discrimination

It would be incorrect to say that the continuing presence of such economic inequality is entirely the result of overt or systemic discrimination or that affirmative action alone would improve the economic position of minorities. But there is no question that

Bob Englehart, *The Hartford Courant*, reprinted with permission.

much of the income and employment disadvantage of blacks and other minorities reflects the accumulated impact of past discrimination. The continuing presence of many seemingly objective policies in the workplace have also had disproportionately unfavorable effects on the hiring, training and upgrading of minority-group workers. Affirmative action has an important role to play in correcting inequities.

In 1969, black workers represented 6.7 percent of the nearly 600,000 employees in the Bell System, mostly black women employed as telephone operators. Only 24 percent of Bell's black employees were in management (compared with 12 percent of whites), 7.2 percent were skilled craftsmen (compared with 26 percent of whites), and less than one percent were in professional jobs (compared with 8 percent of whites).

In 1971, the Equal Employment Opportunity Commission (EEOC) charged AT&T and its affiliates with discrimination against minorities and women. In 1975, after prolonged litigation and negotiations, EEOC and AT&T signed a consent decree designed to correct the inequities in the company's employment practices, and to provide back pay to many minority and female employees who had not enjoyed full equal opportunity in the past. In 1979, blacks and other minorities accounted for 14.4 percent of the Bell System's managerial employees, 18.7 percent of the outside craftsmen, 19.1 percent of the inside craftsmen, and 23.3 percent of the sales workers.

The consent decree was the catalyst necessary to spur the company toward many positive changes in personnel policies that top management today lauds as beneficial to the firm. The more efficient and equitable personnel selection and assessment system adopted by AT&T and its Bell operating affiliates puts the telephone company in a much stronger position to compete with other firms in the increasingly difficult and complex information systems markets. The experience of AT&T, and other firms specifically identified as subjects for affirmative action enforcement, is instructive for understanding the potential impact of affirmative action on the occupational status of minorities. For purposes of public policy formulation, such evidence may be more useful than inconclusive studies that attempt to show the relationship between affirmative action and minority employment opportunities.

"Racial antipathy and discrimination do not explain all that they are purported to explain."

Affirmative Action Is Economically Unnecessary

Walter E. Williams

Walter E. Williams is a professor of economics at George Mason University in Fairfax, Virginia. In 1975, while a National Fellow at the Hoover Institution on War, Peace and Revolution at Stanford University, he began research for his book *The State Against Blacks*. In the following viewpoint, excerpted from that work, Mr. Williams illustrates his belief that it is not affirmative action that is needed to advance minorities, but rather the loosening of governmental restrictions.

As you read, consider the following questions:

1. Why does Mr. Williams think that there aren't any "nice" public schools in the ghettos?
2. How, according to Mr. Williams, did poor blacks infiltrate city neighborhoods?
3. What kind of laws are antipeople, in Mr. Williams' opinion?

Walter E. Williams, *The State Against Blacks*. New York: McGraw-Hill Book Company, 1982. Reprinted with permission.

Racial antipathy and discrimination do not explain all that they are purported to explain. The fact that a person *likes* one race over another does not tell us what that person will find to be in his interests. This is just as true as in the case of anything else. Knowledge that some people like Rolls-Royces better than Pintos or twenty-five point diamonds better than two-point diamonds, alone, cannot unambiguously tell us which the person will possess. To understand fully what people will in fact do, one not only needs to know what people desire, one also needs to know the costs that people must pay for the desired object in question.

All economic evidence shows that the lower the cost of doing something, the more people will do it. Very often the government lowers the costs involved. When the government fixes prices, wages, profits or rents, the tendency for choices to be made on noneconomic criteria increases. Race, sex, national origin are all noneconomic criteria....

The reason why blacks are disadvantaged because of government intervention is no mystery. There is a kind of parity in the marketplace that does not exist in the political arena. Discriminated-against people generally do better under a system where there is market allocation of goods and services than where there is political allocation of goods and services. The market resembles one-man-one-vote. This means that one person's one dollar is the same as another person's one dollar. The difference between people lies in the number of dollars they have. No such parity exists in the political arena.

Markets Determine Possibilities

When choices are made in the market arena, people, including poor people, have a higher probability of getting *some* of what they want, even if they are a minority. When choices are made through the political arena, they very well may get *none* of what they want. That is, if the majority votes to use social resources to produce X and the minority voted for Y, if majority rule carries the day, there will be no Y.

Partial evidence of this, as Dr. Milton Friedman points out, is seen in the poorest ghettos of the nation. If you go through the ghetto, you will see *some* nice clothing and *some* nice foods. In that respect the residents have *some* of the things that middle-class and rich people possess. But you will see no nice public schools. Why not at least *some* public schools like rich people have? Cars, clothing and food are distributed by the market mechanism. Schools are distributed by the political mechanism. More often than not, if a nice school is found in the ghetto, it is a nonpublic school.

The power of the market is seen when one looks at the historical housing opportunities for blacks. Appreciation of the market ability to thwart the forces of racial discrimination is gained by asking the following question: How did blacks seize the use-control of housing in the central areas of most major cities? During the racially hostile times of the 1920s, 30s, 40s, one could not prevent whole blocks and neighborhoods from going from white to black virtually overnight. The fact ought to give rise to the question: How did poor, discriminated-against-blacks do this? Keep in mind that some of these neighborhoods were occupied by relatively affluent whites.

Poor Outbid the Nonpoor

The poor blacks simply outbid the whites for the property. At first thought, the ability of poor people to outbid nonpoor people may seem an impossibility. But an example can show how it is possible. Imagine a three-story brownstone being rented by a nonpoor white family for $200 per month. Suppose further that the landlord does not like blacks. But if six poor black families suggested that the building be partitioned into six parts to rent for $75 per part, the landlord might have to reassess his position. Namely, he would have to evaluate the prospect of an income yield of $450, by renting to the six blacks, as opposed to an income yield of $200 by retaining his white tenant. The fact that blacks have come to occupy neighborhoods formerly occupied by whites demonstrates that the landlord's dilemma was resolved in favor of blacks.

Real Economic Setbacks for Blacks

While liberals ignore issues of real concern to blacks, government wages a silent war on the aspirations of black people. Zoning laws are used to prevent the spread of multi-family housing, thus restricting poor blacks to ghettos far from potential jobs. Licensing laws keep blacks from getting jobs as cab drivers in New York City or as truck drivers on interstate routes. As the National Conference of Black Mayors recently recognized, the minimum wage law is used to prevent blacks from entering the job market—exactly the way it is used in South Africa.

Richard A. Viguerie, "Liberals Versus Blacks," *Conservative Digest,* March 1984.

Now the question: Why is it that poor blacks did not inundate suburban areas to the extent they did the cities? The answer is easy: The power of the state subverted the operation of the market. Suburban areas, to a greater extent than cities, have highly restrictive zoning ordinances. There are laws that fix the minimum lot size, minimum floor space in the house, minimum distance to adjacent houses plus laws that restrict property use to a single family. The combined effect of these laws, independent of *de jure* or *de facto* racial discrimination, is to deny poor people the chance to outbid nonpoor people. It is far more difficult for a person to get together the whole house price than one month's rent for a cubbyhole.

Offsetting Discrimination

Herein lies the power of the market. People can offset some of their handicaps by offering a higher price for what they buy or a lower price for what they sell. Many well-meaning people are morally outraged by such a necessity. But the fact of business is that if handicapped people are not permitted to use price as a bargaining tool, they may very well end up with none of what they want as opposed to some.

There are numerous laws, regulations and ordinances that have reduced or eliminated avenues of upward mobility for blacks. The common feature of these barriers is that they prevent people from making transactions that are deemed mutually beneficial by the *transactors*. However, it would be extremely misleading to leave the reader with the impression that these laws are exclusively antiblack. An ordinance that generates a $60,000 license price to own a taxi, such as the one in New York City, discriminates and handicaps *anyone*, brown, black, white or yellow, who cannot meet the price. Therefore, these laws are antipeople! They are only antiblack to the extent that blacks may be least likely to meet the entry conditions. Blacks were the last major ethnic group to become urbanized and to gain basic civil rights. When they finally achieved that status, blacks found that new barriers had been erected.

Antipeople Laws

Laws that restrict economic activity are antipeople in another way. Another effect of these laws is they *always* raise prices and often reduce the received quality of the regulated good or service. This makes for a lower standard of living than would be the case with less restrictive licensing and regulation. On top of this, American citizens are made to suffer in two additional ways. Because of restricted economic opportunities more people than otherwise would be the case are living at taxpayer expense through welfare, unemployment compensation and other income supplemental programs. Moreover, when we are called to support the indigent the support level is higher because of the higher product prices caused by the monopolistic restrictions.

Our recognition that laws which create economic barriers are antipeople is important, not for analytical clarity alone, but for another reason as well. Such a recognition may suggest political strategy for change. The people who financially benefit from New York's taxicab monopoly, for example, are relatively few in number. The beneficiaries are taxi owners and those in allied trades. The people who bear the burden of the monopoly are large in number. They are the taxicab riders of New York City, who receive a lower quality service and pay higher prices, and all those who would enter the taxi business.

Eliminating Monopolies

Such a tabulation of beneficiaries and losers of New York's taxi monopoly suggests that a political coalition could be formed to eliminate the monopoly. A coalition of voters could be formed to counter the political pressure by the Teamsters Union and taxi owner associations to maintain and enhance the monopoly. Moreover, the recognition that government-sponsored monopolies are antipeople tells us that blacks, who are already taxi owners, are part of the opposition. People like a monopoly in what they sell. Black people are not immune to this propensity. Blacks who are a part of a monopolized market structure, such as a licensed trade or occupation or a union-protected job, will share the same interest in monopoly maintenance as whites.

Economically the solution to problems of upward mobility that blacks face are relatively simple. Their most difficult problem lies in the political arena. How can they eliminate or reduce the power of interest groups to use government to exclude? The broad solution to exclusion for all Americans is for the United States Supreme Court to interpret the right to work as it now interprets the right to speech. The Court has all but said that there is no compelling state reason for limiting freedom of speech. Similarly, there are very few compelling state reasons for limiting the freedom to work.

Understanding Words in Context

Readers occasionally come across words which they do not recognize. And freqently, because the reader does not know a word or words, he or she will not fully understand the passage being read. Obviously, the reader can look up an unfamiliar word in a dictionary. However, by carefully examining the word in the context in which it is used, the word's meaning can often be determined. A careful reader may find clues to the meaning of the word in surrounding words, ideas and attitudes.

Below are statements taken from the viewpoints in this chapter. In each statement one or two words are printed in italics. Try to determine the meaning of each word by reading the excerpt. Under each statement you will find four definitions for the italicized word. Choose the one that is closest to your understanding of the word.

Finally, use a dictionary to see how well you have understood the words in context. It will be helpful to discuss with others the clues which helped you decide each word's meaning.

1. Debate over the *VALIDITY* of affirmative action as a strategy for redressing some of the *INEQUITIES* of society has begun again.

    VALIDITY means:
    a) soundness   b) tragedy
    c) necessity   d) wrongness

    INEQUITIES means:
    a) indignities   b) unfairness
    c) beliefs   d) needs

2. Current impatience with affirmative action may *DERIVE* from the *NARCISSISM* of the culture: Fewer people hold philosophical and religious beliefs that make them feel responsible to do something about institutionalized prejudice.

    DERIVE means:
    a) be concluded   b) happen suddenly
    c) originate   d) be expected to happen

NARCISSISM means:
a) sadness
b) vulgarity
c) rudeness
d) egotism

3. Affirmative action as that term was originally used and understood carried with it no *CONNOTATION* of *PREFERENTIAL* treatment.

CONNOTATION means:
a) jargon
b) suggestion
c) decision
d) basis

PREFERENTIAL means:
a) to prefer
b) to exclude
c) to reject
d) to discriminate

4. Why has society selected one kind of wrong—discrimination—as particularly deserving or demanding *RECTIFICATION*?

RECTIFICATION means:
a) improvement
b) attention
c) destroy
d) qualification

5. Denying a man a job on grounds of color is evidently just one among many ways of wronging him. It is far less *EGREGIOUS* than assault or murder.

EGREGIOUS means:
a) agreeable
b) customary
c) monstrous
d) unusual

6. Examination of statistics bears out the claim that discriminatory practices of the past continue to have concrete *MANIFESTATIONS* today.

MANIFESTATIONS means:
a) impact
b) demonstrations
c) ideals
d) intent

7. Racial *ANTIPATHY* and discrimination do not explain all that they are purported to explain.

ANTIPATHY means:
a) indifference
b) harmony
c) affection
d) hatred

8. We must not avoid the moral issues by further debate about the moral or legal acceptability of *REPARATIONS* to the victims of American exploitation.

REPARATIONS means:
a) compensation
b) payment
c) gifts
d) jobs

Periodical Bibliography

The following list of periodical articles deals with the subject matter of this chapter.

Carl Cohen
"Why Racial Preference is Illegal and Immoral," *Commentary*, June 1979.

Conservative Digest
"What Conservatives Would Do for Minorities," March 1984.

Robert F. Drinan
"Affirmative Action Under Attack," *America*, February 4, 1984.

Andrew Greeley
"Ethnic's Progress: Is Data Fact?" *Psychology Today*, September 1981.

Walter Guzzardi Jr.
"The Right to Strive for Equality," *Fortune*, March 9, 1981.

Christopher Hitchens
"Minority Report," *The Nation*, October 16, 1982.

Michael Kinsley
"Equal Lack of Opportunity," *Harper's*, June 1983.

Harvey C. Mansfield
"The Underhandedness of Affirmative Action," *National Review*, May 4, 1984.

Thomas Nagel
"Caste Struggle," *New Republic*, January 23, 1984.

National Review
"Reverse Reverse Discrimination," February 4, 1983.

The New York Times
"Just How Fair Is Affirmative Action? A Debate: William Bradford Reynolds and Drew S. Days III," December 11, 1983.

Dirk Olin
"Equal Opportunities," *New Republic*, May 30, 1983.

Daniel Seligman
"Affirmative Action Is Here to Stay," *Fortune*, April 19, 1982.

Thomas Sowell
"Myths about Minorities," *Commentary*, August 1979.

USA Today
"The War Has Not Yet Been Won," December 1983.

US News & World Report
"Job Discrimination Is Still Very, Very Serious," March 14, 1983.

Are the Poor
Treated Fairly?

"Until we establish the right to income with dignity, millions of Americans will continue to suffer needless deprivation."

The Poor Are Not Treated Fairly

Food First

Food First is sponsored by the Institute for Food and Development Policy in San Francisco, California. The organization seeks to provide people with the information and material necessary to take back control of their food resources. It functions to create social, economic, and political structures that ensure food security for all. In the following viewpoint, Food First insists that the poor are being treated unfairly in America. Poor Americans are being robbed of their economic rights, and a reduction in inflation can in no way compensate for these rights.

As you read, consider the following questions:

1. According to the author, what are the three economic rights "that ought to be guaranteed for all Americans"?
2. How do the Fortune 500 corporations use their wealth, according to the authors?
3. How, do the authors suggest, can we eliminate poverty and hunger in America?

"Don't Just Blame Reagan," a Food First Action Alert published in June 1983 by The Institute for Food and Development Policy, 1885 Mission Street, San Francisco, CA 94103. Reprinted with permission.

Across the United States, soup kitchens are swamped with people who once had jobs but now can't even afford to feed their families.

"I've worked hard all my life and didn't ask to be laid off," a jobless veteran from Indianapolis told a Senate committee. "We desperately need some help right now. The president's cutting back on food stamps really scares me."

"We lost our funding for lunches," a day-care teacher explained to a hunger-action group in Los Angeles. "Now at lunchtime I see the children running out to the parking lot—they're fighting over food out of the garbage cans."

Twice as many people as last year are coming to church basement soup kitchens and community food banks. Yet North American farmers have record harvests and supermarket shelves boast an abundance of food. Why, then, are so many people hungry in this rich country?

Poverty Is a Major Problem

As in Bangladesh, the problem is not scarcity: it's poverty. According to the Census Bureau, more than 31 million Americans—one out of seven—are living in poverty. It's worse for children: one in five lives below the poverty line. Twelve million Americans are officially out of work and another 1.8 million have given up looking. Over 6 million can't find as much work as they want; others work full time for the minimum wage—$3.35 per hour—and still can't support their families. Four out of five black teenagers can't find jobs.

Meanwhile, the Reagan administration has made the largest cuts in social benefits in history—just when hundreds of thousands of previously employed Americans are joining the ranks of the "new poor." Food stamps make it easier for poor people to eat decently, yet under Reaganomics, 1 million people have been kicked out of the program and another 20 million have had their benefits cut.

The president claimed that his program of tax cuts for the corporations and the wealthy and deregulation of business would get the economy moving again. But while inflation and interest rates are going down, even his own economists predict continued double-digit unemployment this year. "President Reagan's dream of quick transition to 'a brighter future for all our citizens' has become a nightmare of unemployment and bankruptcy for many Americans," concludes the *Wall Street Journal*.

This recession, the longest since World War II, is not like previous ones. Millions of laid-off workers will never be rehired because their industries, such as auto and steel, are shrinking. Although they produce the greatest abundance in history, they are devastated by low prices, soaring costs, and increasing concentration of farm ownership. Farm bankruptcy rates are the highest since the Great Depression. Housing prices are out of reach for most Americans, and the Social Security System that many older people depend on seems to be in trouble.

Failure to Change Poverty Structures

In fact, most Americans are losing ground. Over the last decade, the purchasing power of the average worker's earnings has shrunk 16 percent. The U.S. economy, which offered an ever-increasing standard of living for several generations is disappointing a lot of their children.

While President Reagan's programs have made things worse, earlier economic plans also failed to eliminate hunger and poverty. That's because neither economic expansion nor the government programs tried so far have ever created enough jobs for all who want to work—or economic security for those who can't provide for themselves (such as children or people unable to work). The social programs introduced in the sixties and seventies, such as food stamps and school lunch programs, did reduce hunger. But they couldn't get to the root of American poverty because they refused to alter the structures that keep so many Americans poor and disenfranchised.

The failure of past programs to change these structures, and the economic crises we face today, bring us to a crossroads, an opportunity to try a new approach. By establishing our economic rights, we could use our vast material wealth and human energies to end hunger and poverty and create a new, more democratic economy that would better serve all Americans.

Guaranteed Economic Rights

But what are these economic rights that ought to be guaranteed for all Americans?

1. The right to a decent job with decent pay. Without this right, even those who are working now will have no security. In the last two years, over 1 million people lost their jobs due to plant closings. Millions of Americans work full time for the minimum wage and still can't get by. (Could you support a family of four on $3.35 an hour—about $540 a month?)

Until a decent job is a right, guaranteed with government help if necessary, joblessness will continue to dash the dreams of millions. With more than 12 million of us officially out of work, the unemployment rate today is triple what was considered acceptable in the 1960s.

2. The right of income with dignity for those out of work or unable to work. Without this right, there's no guarantee that people in need will get unemployment insurance or welfare payments or that this aid will cover their basic needs. While many jobless Europeans receive 80 percent of their regular pay when they're laid off, the average American gets only half. And regardless of our needs, the size and duration of benefits can be cut at any time—as they have under the Reagan administration. Despite the highest unemployment in four decades, only 41 percent of jobless Americans are getting unemployment benefits, compared to 60 percent during the 1975 recession.

Many Americans are unable to work—even if jobs were available—because they are too old, too sick, or taking care of children. Yet Social Security payments are inadequate for many elderly people and only about half those eligible get food stamps. And in no state do welfare payments and food stamps combined even bring families up to the poverty line. Until we establish the right to income with dignity, millions of Americans will continue to suffer needless deprivation and indignity, no matter how high the Dow Jones goes.

The Reality of the Working Poor

The loaded label of "underclass" obscures the reality of the working poor in the United States, who increasingly are forced into low-paying, dead end jobs. As the American economy continues to generate more secondary and fewer primary jobs...the situation of inadequate income, instable work, and hustling to get over may come to characterize the working life of many more Americans. The debate on urban poverty should direct our attention to the profound changes occurring in the economy, and to the need for fundamental changes in labor market structure.

Rick McGahey, "In Search of the Undeserving Poor," *Working Papers*, November/December 1981.

---

3. The right to participate in democratic decisions about how the nation's resources are used. While we accept as a given our right to vote on many political issues, we've come to accept as normal and natural that a few thousand men in corporate boardrooms make most of the key economic decisions. We invest our work, our savings, our pension funds to create our country's wealth, but we let others have the final word about our pay, about our health, safety, and working conditions, about whether the factory where we work should be shut down and moved to Taiwan or the Philippines.

Should American factories produce more cars, or should we use the same resources to build a new train system? Should we spend billions on an MX missile system that not even the Joint Chiefs of Staff agree on, or should we use the money to rebuild our cities? Without more democratic participation in decision-making on such key economic issues, corporate executives and the legislators who go along with them will continue to make the big decisions for us.

In the United States, five hundred corporations control over 80 percent of all industrial assets, and this concentration of control is increasing every year. The richest one half of 1 percent of Americans control half of all privately owned corporate stock. American consumers are overcharged $20 billion a year because of monopoly in the food industry. The Fortune 500 corporations use their wealth both to influence the political process and to shape our very understanding of democracy—so that we don't even think in terms of economic rights.

Today we're paying for the bad decisions an elite group of corporate planners has made, thanks to what Reagan calls "the magic of the marketplace." Naturally enough, corporate planners make their decisions in their interests—short-term profits and corporate growth—not ours. Instead of investing in useful, job-creating production, they decided to spend over $136 billion on mergers in the last two years, creating no jobs and drying up credit that smaller businesses needed just to stay afloat. In the last year alone they decided to bring us 2,400 new food products—including 58 new salad dressings and 125 "light" foods—when some Americans could afford only dog food. They decided to continue to build big, gas-guzzling cars while more and more Americans were switching to small cars imported from Japan or Europe. They decided to develop expensive, dangerous nuclear power, when we needed greater emphasis on conservation and solar power.

Over the past thirty years, business interests have used their political power to reduce their share of taxes by 62 percent, while individuals are paying 28 percent more. Early in the Reagan administration, a congressional committee voted cuts in corporate income taxes worth $500 billion over the next decade. Small wonder: thirty of the committee's thirty-five members had received corporate contributions totaling $1,739,119 for their 1980 campaigns.

"Free" Market Not So Free

The corporate message, communicated through advertising, free classroom materials, corporate-financed "think tanks," and politicians is simple: the economy works best when people keep their hands off and the "laws" of the marketplace are liberated. Only a "free market"—that is, one they control—is consistent with political liberty.

But political liberty flourishes and people live more secure lives in some other nations whose citizens have already started claiming their economic rights. In France, England, and Denmark, for example, health care is a right. In Sweden, voters recently elected a party proposing that workers buy into ownership of major corporations so they can begin to set corporate priorities that make sense for workers too. While these advances are very limited, they are steps in the right direction.

Now we too must take steps toward an Economic Bill of Rights, because an economy constructed around these rights could provide more democratic control over the economy and economic security for every American. While no one has a blueprint, people around the world are exploring innovative ways to build stronger, more just economies that meet the needs of all their citizens. We Americans can also devise new ways to claim our economic rights....

It's tempting to react to the current economic crisis with despair, even cynicism, given the callous economic strategies of our corporate and government leaders. But remember that if economic rights seem like a dream to us now, less than one hundred years ago a guaranteed minimum wage, the right to vote for women, and the right to form labor unions also seemed out of reach.

We must keep alive a sense of outrage, remembering the children suffering from hunger amidst record harvests, the skilled workers standing in soup lines, the old people who can only afford one meal a day. As the links between political and economic power are revealed ever more starkly, we can make the 1980s a time when millions not only come to see their economic rights as essential to democracy but move forward to claim them. Then we can finally end poverty and hunger in our country.

"The poorest, who have benefited the most from the reduction in inflation, have also been the least affected by the [budget] cuts."

The Poor Are Treated Fairly

Michael Novak

Michael Novak is a resident scholar in philosophy, religion and public policy at the American Enterprise Institute. He is the author of *The Rise of the Unmeltable Ethnics, The Spirit of Democratic Capitalism,* and *Confessions of a Catholic.* In the following viewpoint, Mr. Novak discusses what he believes are myths about the causes of poverty in America, and how poverty should not be a "fairness" issue.

As you read, consider the following questions:

1. According to Mr. Novak, do the rich benefit from tax cuts? Why or why not?
2. What does Mr. Novak mean by his claim that the poor are making "more honest dollars" under the Reagan administration?
3. What "new" solutions does Mr. Novak suggest to eliminate poverty in America?

Michael Novak, "The Rich, the Poor, & the Reagan Administration." Reprinted from *Commentary,* August 1983, by permission; all rights reserved.

According to a recent Gallup poll, 82 percent of the American people hold that President Reagan's domestic programs "help the rich" and 75 percent hold that they "hurt the poor."...

When one tries to establish what is "fair," problems arise immediately. In 1976, Jimmy Carter campaigned on the claim that the tax system of the U.S. was so unfair as to constitute "a disgrace to the human race." By 1980, no one thought that Carter, as President, had made it less so. As he departed office, Carter also left behind an annual rate of inflation of 13 percent, 7.5 percent unemployment, interest rates at 22 percent. No one then claimed that Carter was helping the poor. By his own description, the country was suffering a broad "malaise." It is by no means obvious, then, that Reagan's programs are any more unfair than Carter's.

Appealing to Class Conflict

Some religious spokesmen...will insist that through control and further regulatory legislation, all poverty can be eliminated. They favor forced redistribution of wealth. They find all poverty as the result of injustice on the part of the rich, and thereby appeal to the temptation to class conflict.

We are not in dangerous times today because our economy is worse than it has ever been. It is not, nor even near it. We are in the most dangerous times today because there are those who are willing to take advantage of any difficulty, any disaster, any appetites for the destruction of the noble and the good."

Frank Morriss, "Lack of Virtue, Not Jobs, At Root of Social Unrest," *The Wanderer,* December 16, 1982.

What is obvious, however, is that the Reagan administration's critics have more exalted standards in mind. Some judge fairness by the degree of "redistribution" effected in society. In their eyes, an administration would be fair if it took from the rich and gave to the poor. Yet as Bertrand de Jouvenal long ago pointed out, this dreamy ideal can never be fulfilled literally, for the simple mathematical reason that there are too few rich and that, even in the aggregate, they have too little income. The most recent Internal Revenue Service tables (for 1980) could hardly be clearer on this point: only 117,000 Americans had a gross adjusted income of $200,000 or more. Their total income came to $46 billion, on which they paid $20 billion (or 43 percent) in income taxes. To confiscate the entire remaining after-tax income of every U.S. citizen earning over $200,000 and give it all to the poor, whatever one might say about the "fairness" of such a measure, would result in under $850 for each individual officially counted as poor....

The record of tax payments to the IRS is not well-known. Here are the tables for 1980:

Personal Income Taxes Paid, 1980
(money amounts in billions)

IRS Income Groups	Number of Returns	Gross Adjusted Income	Total Taxes	% of All Taxes Paid
Total:	93,902,469	$1,613.7	$250.3	100
$0-5,000	20,055,529	49.7	.07	0.3
5-10,000	18,370,997	136.6	7.8	3.1
10-15,000	14,303,041	177.1	17.1	6.8
15-50,000	38,043,711	992.7	146.2	58.4
50,000-100,000	2,568,427	165.9	39.8	15.9
100,000-200,000	443,514	58.6	19.4	7.6
200,000+	117,250	45.8	19.5	7.8

As the figures suggest, those Americans who earned more than $50,000 in 1980—the top 3 percent—remitted 31 percent of all income taxes paid, or 79 billion of the total $250 billion collected by the IRS from individual income taxes. In 1980, the bottom 50 percent, or those who made $12,000 or less, paid $14 billion in income tax (or only 6 percent of all taxes paid). Thus, the top 3 percent paid five times more in taxes than the bottom 50 percent combined.

For the top 3 percent to carry the bottom 50 percent seems highly admirable. What one cannot say is that those in the top layer "benefit" unduly from a cut in tax rates that is of the exact proportion granted to every other taxpayer. For by saying this one would simply be calling attention to the far greater proportion of taxes such persons are now paying. The Reagan tax cuts of 1981 were, by design, one and the same for all, at every income level. In fact, as the independent Congressional Budget Office has noted, under the Reagan program "the largest tax cut in dollar terms" has gone not to the very rich but to the "$10,000 to $40,000 middle-income group, which as a group also has the most households and the most income." The CBO adds: "The highest category (of income earners) receives a slightly lower cut relative to previous tax liability." This is because for such persons the topmost 50 percent marginal rate on earned income remains in effect....

Not only have high-income persons not benefited disproportionately from the cut in tax rates, but the gross amount they are paying is, if anything, greater than before the cuts went into effect....

If the "rich" side of the so-called "fairness" issue seems to have less in it than meets the eye, what about the "poor" side? Is President Reagan's program hurting the poor?

In one area—employment—the obvious answer is yes. Although one cannot blame Reagan for an unemployment rate already going up well before his tax and welfare programs went into effect, the fact that unemployment rose by a full 3 percent during Reagan's first two years in office means that some 3 million families experienced real hardship. Savings were wiped out; lifetime projects were grievously interrupted or destroyed; fears spread; some factory doors clanged shut forever.

Yet when people say that Reagan's programs are hurting the poor they have in mind not so much the number of the unemployed as the condition of the welfare programs sustaining the poor. Quite apart from the increase in the numbers of the poor because of unemployment, the poor are said to be getting poorer.

The Meaning of "Cuts"

President Reagan is alleged to be cutting benefits to the poor. But what does "cutting" mean? One can cut a benefit in three ways: (a) by inflation; (b) by providing less funding; (c) by curbing a projected growth in funding. For Democrats, the classic way of cutting benefits has been to give with one hand (in appropriations) while taking away with the other (through inflation). This was President Carter's way. During his four years in office, inflation raged almost at double-digit levels for three years, devastating individuals and families with low income or fixed income. Inflation is the cruelest tax, although the easiest one for the "party of compassion" to levy. (To adapt an old Tammany Hall saying: "The fella who said, 'Patriotism is the last refuge of scoundrels' overlooked the possibilities of compassion.") President Carter levied the tax of inflation with a vengeance.

In this respect, Reagan has done more to *help* the poor than Carter. Inflation has come down more quickly, more steeply and (so far) more steadily than anyone dared to hope on inauguration day. Whatever dollars the poor receive under Reagan, they are more honest dollars than they were under Carter, when even the practice of indexing welfare benefits to the rate of inflation could not prevent all other costs from leaping beyond reach.

As for gross expenditures on welfare programs, even adjusting for inflation, there are a few—but only a few—welfare programs on which the government is spending less in 1983 under Reagan than was spent in 1980 under Carter. In the aggregate, certainly, far *more* is being spent. Even in 1980, critics said welfare spending was "out of control." It still is. Mercilessly, and most often without commensurate benefit, it just keeps going up, automatically. President Reagan deserves little "credit" for this; on the contrary, he has tried desperately to control it. Yet his efforts to make deep cuts have by and large failed....

Take the three biggest items, the so-called "middle-class" social programs which actually benefit the poor even more significantly than they benefit others: Social Security, Medicare, and Medicaid. (Poverty was not long ago a problem predominantly of the elderly; these three programs have virtually ended that.) On these three programs Reagan is indisputably spending more than Carter did:

Outlays for Three Basic Social Programs
(millions of dollars)

	1980	1983
Social Security	117,117	168,267
Medicare	35,033	57,262
Medicaid	13,956	19,326
Total:	116,106	244,875

[Source: Office of Management and Budget]

Thus, the sharpest accusations about "hurting the poor" cannot plausibly be aimed at these three fundamental welfare programs. But what about the relatively minor programs designed especially for the poor: Aid for Families with Dependent Children (AFDC), food stamps, housing assistance, rent supplements, Small Business Administration minority loan programs, Head Start, and the long list of other agencies, programs and benefits? These amount, in aggregate, to about 10 percent of all federal spending, or some $70 billion. And it is on these that the case against Reagan rests.

This case is built principally on the contention that the administration has not merely cut the rate of increase of the programs in question, but has also made actual inroads into their funding. The particulars, which tend to bear out the President's frequent assertion that virtually every program has been budgeted for more in 1983 than in 1980, speak for themselves:

Outlays for Social Programs
(millions of dollars)

	1980	Estimated 1983
Unemployment Benefits	18,029.2	36,855.0
Housing Programs	5,353.6	9,325.0
Food Stamps	9,117.1	12,0451.1
Child Nutrition	3,377.1	3,196.5
Women, Infants, Children	716.7	1,117.7
AFDC	7,308.4	7,766.8
Supplemental Security Income	6,411.5	8,845.3
Earned Income Tax Credit	1,275.2	1,205.0

[Source: Office of Management and Budget]

These figures are not adjusted for inflation (which has been reduced but not eliminated). In a time of recession, moreover, one would expect to see a gross increase in social spending to ease the burden of the poor and near-poor. Just such an increase is patent in these figures. Still, some categories show only a slight rise or, in two cases, a fall. The fact that the Reagan administration has tightened eligibility requirements for these programs just at this precise moment is the most plausible reason for saying that Reagan's program is unfair.

On whom did these cuts fall most heavily? Not on the poorest of the poor. By all evidence, the poorest, who have benefited the most from the reduction in inflation, have also been the least affected by the Reagan cuts. In every category, those cut have been at the *top* of the relevant criteria for eligibility. So much is this the case that some conservatives and liberals have jointly rebelled, calling it a scandal that the Reagan "ax" has fallen most harshly on the "working poor," those on the upper boundaries of poverty and dependence. Are these not the very persons—so to speak, the "most deserving" poor—who ought to be encouraged? Why cut

Michael Novak

off *their* benefits? Except that just above their ranks there are others who also could use a little extra help, and also above those. (Moreover, under previous practices, 80 percent of the "working poor" were *not* receiving the benefits received by a lucky 20 percent; *this* unfairness more than any other has brought welfare into disrepute.)

It is thus a portion of the borderline poor who have felt the pain. Within those programs which have been cut, or whose growth has been cut, the Reagan policies have consistently aimed at removing from the rolls those with higher incomes. Ironically, these are the very ones among the poor likely to have voted for Reagan in 1980, and presumably likely to do so again in 1984, in numbers much greater than the poorest of the poor, whose eligibility has been entirely protected. As Roosevelt is sometimes referred to as the liberal who saved capitalism, Reagan may some day be known as the conservative who saved the welfare state intact for the very poor.

Welfare Ranks Swelling

If, however, the Reagan administration has neither helped the rich nor hurt the poor in the blatant way that has been charged by its critics, it *has* failed to address meaningfully the larger question posed by the continuing existence of a welfare population whose ranks are not diminishing but appear rather to be swelling.

Federal expenditures for human services no longer seem to be correlated with decreases in the level of poverty. More money is being spent; poverty seems not to have been reduced. In constant, uninflated dollars, and adjusted for population increases, government spent seven times as much on direct cash-income transfers in 1970 as in 1950. It then spent twice as much in 1980 as in 1970. In addition, many in-kind transfers (food stamps, housing assistance, Medicaid) increased dramatically.

It is true that, thanks mainly to the rapid economic growth of the 60's, and perhaps also to Lyndon Johnson's "War on Poverty," the percentage of the population in poverty dropped from about 30 percent in 1950 to under 12 percent in the early 1970's; but then it began to grow again, and in a manner utterly unresponsive to federal ministrations.

In the latest year for which numbers are available (1981), there were 31 million poor persons, defined as all those in non-farm families of four having an income lower than $9,287. Of these, significantly more than half, almost 17 million, were under age sixteen, mostly the children of single mothers. Only a small proportion—about 3 million—were over sixty-five. Thus, only about 11 million of the poor fall between the ages of sixteen and sixty-five and are therefore capable of being active in the market system on their own behalf. A significant portion of these adults, moreover, are single mothers; others are handicapped, ill, or otherwise afflicted. This leaves only a small number, about 2 million, of able-bodied persons who can work.

Obviously, a decent society wants to put a solid financial floor under all its citizens who cannot help themselves or who are temporarily down on their luck. (For the vast majority of the poor, a poverty income occurs only in one or two years out of ten; it is rarely a permanent condition.) Given the figures above, how much would it cost to do this?

For the sake of simplicity, let us stipulate that there are 8 million poor households (dividing 31 million individuals into households of four), and that, on average, each of these households has about $4,500 of income. Then, in order to gauge the magnitude of the "problem" of poverty, we might multiply the number of poor households by $5,000 (the difference, roughly, between the stipulated average income and the official cut-off figure of $9,287). It does not seem from this perspective that financing every non-farm family of four at a minimum floor would cost more than $40 billion. Even if the 8 million poor households had no income of their own (except guaranteed medical care), the cost would not be more than $75 billion. Seen in this light, and defined solely in monetary terms (as the poverty "industry" does define it), poverty is not an especially expensive problem.

The Poor Are Always With Us

There will always be a few hungry people. Many of the hungry were rejected from mental institutions. Their problem is not lack of food, but inability to take care of themselves. And the fact that 50 people eat at a soup kitchen doesn't mean that we should make another five million people eligible for food stamps.

James Bovard, "Stop the Hysteria Over a Hungry Few," *USA Today,* April 2, 1984.

In 1983, the federal government will spend not $40 billion but an estimated $400 billion in entitlements to individuals. As we have noted, most of this ($244.8 billion) is granted through Social Security, Medicare, and Medicaid. But a rather substantial portion is also granted through the multiple programs mentioned above: food stamps; AFDA; low-income housing or rent supplements; the supplemental food program for women, infants and children; school-lunch programs; and the like. Would it not be cheaper, more efficient, and ultimately more successful to eliminate these minor programs and give sufficient funds directly to the poor, in order to lift them above the federally defined poverty level?

This leads to another question: does not the current design of programs afford "mischievous" incentives, increasing rather than decreasing the number of the poor from year to year? There is strong evidence that this is what is occurring. The widely noticed "feminization of poverty" is a case in point. As distinct from twenty years ago, a large majority of the poor today consists of single mothers and their children. From year to year, these numbers have recently begun to accelerate.

American People's Generosity

The American people have been exceedingly generous in the amounts of money they have assigned for the elimination of poverty; yet, despite this expenditure, poverty seems not on the way to being eliminated but rather to be growing. Surely, therefore, it is incumbent on all of us—but especially on those who accuse President Reagan of "hurting the poor"—to think of alternatives.

"The overwhelming majority of the poor are poor because they have, first: insufficient income; and second: no access to methods of increasing that income."

The Poor Need Outside Help

William Ryan

William Ryan is currently a professor of psychology at Boston College. A clinical psychologist by training, he received his Ph.D. from Boston University. Dr. Ryan has been active in the areas of welfare rights and prison reform since the mid-1960s and helped organize the Citizen Observer Program in Walpole Prison in 1973. He is the author of *Distress in the City, Blaming the Victim,* and *Equality.* In the following viewpoint, Dr. Ryan examines the plight of the poor and concludes that the poor remain poor because they lack the economic mobility that status or family contacts give.

As you read, consider the following questions:

1. What is "the poverty cult" that Dr. Ryan refers to?
2. What is the primary cause of poverty, according to Dr. Ryan?
3. According to the author, how should we tackle the problem of poverty?

William Ryan, *Blaming the Victim.* New York: Pantheon Books, 1976. Reprinted by permission of Pantheon Books, a division of Random House Inc.

There is vast sociological literature detailing the supposed differences between the poor and the middle class on such variables—including values, child-rearing practices, level of aspiration, sexual behavior, and so forth. As in the case of ability to defer gratification, it is found that the middle class come out on top every time—they are said to have greater commitment to education, achievement, orderly family lives, sexual regularity, and to rear their children in such a way as to impel them to do likewise. More recently, these ideas have been pulled together into such packages as the "culture of poverty" and the "lower class culture." And here is where we start to run into ideological trouble. Viewed simply as descriptions, all these different portraits of poor people might simply be dismissed as stereotypes or exaggerations. They might be left to the ministrations of a Poor People's Anti-Defamation League, if there were one. But aficionados of the culture of poverty go several steps further into very dangerous territory. They identify the culture of poverty and lower class culture and the presumed life styles of the poor as themselves *causes* of continued poverty....

Being poor is having no cash in hand and damned little on the way. Put in these terms, poverty in the United States is almost a picayune problem. A redistribution of about fifteen billion dollars a year (less than two per cent of our Gross National Product that is now pushing toward one trillion dollars annually) would bring every poor person above the present poverty line....

Poor Way of Life?

But if poverty is to be understood more clearly in terms of the "way of life" of the poor, in terms of a "lower class culture," as a product of a deviant value system, then money is clearly not the answer. We can stop right now worrying about ways of redistributing our resources more equitably, and begin focusing our concern where it belongs—on the poor themselves. We can start trying to figure out how to change that troublesome culture of theirs, how to apply some tautening astringent to their flabby consciences, how to deal with their poor manners and make them more socially acceptable. By this hard and wearying method of liquidating lower class culture, we can liquidate the lower class, and, thereby, bring an end to poverty....

The concept of culture has been defined many times, and although no definition has achieved universal acceptance, most of the definitions include three central ideas: that culture is passed on from generation to generation, that a culture represents a ready-made prescription for living and for making day-to-day decisions, and, finally, that the components of a culture are accepted by those in the culture as good, and true, and not to be questioned. The eminent anthropologist George Murdock has listed seventy-three items that characterize every known culture, past and present. The list begins with Age-grading and Athletic sports, runs to Weaning and Weather Control, and includes on the way such items as Calendar, Firemaking, Property Rights, and Toolmaking. I would submit that even the most extreme advocate of a culture of poverty viewpoint would readily acknowledge that, with respect to almost all of these items, every American, beyond the first-generation immigrant, regardless of race or class, is a member of a common culture. We all share pretty much the same sports. Maybe poor kids don't know how to play polo, and rich kids don't spend time with stickball, but we all know baseball, and football, and basketball. Despite some misguided efforts to raise minor dialects to the status of separate tongues, we all, in fact, share the same language. There may be differences in diction and usage, but it would be ridiculous to say that all Americans don't speak English. We have the calendar, the law, and large numbers of other cultural items in common. It may well be true that on a few of the seventy-three items there are minor variations between classes, but these kinds of things are really slight variations on a common theme. There are other items that show variability, not in relation to class, but in relation to religion and ethnic background—funeral customs and cooking, for example. But if there is one place in America where the melting pot is a reality, it is on the kitchen stove; in the course of one month, half the readers of this sentence have probably eaten pizza, hot pastrami, and chow mein. Specific differences that might be identified as signs of separate cultural identity are relatively insignificant within the general unity of American life; they are cultural commas and semicolons in the paragraphs and pages of American life.

That the poor in America constitute a separate culture, then, is a manifest absurdity....

How the Poor Differ

The point to be made in this controversy is simply this: if the poor are different in significant ways from the rest of us, are these differences *cultural?* It is easy to be misled and to fall into the easy jargon of the day and call all kinds of minor phenomena cultures or subcultures. Consider a possible analogy: there are several million men who share certain traits, centering around an addiction to alcohol; they work irregularly, for example, show a high arrest rate, and also have high rates of family disorganization; they represent a minority of alcoholics, an even smaller minority of heavy drinkers. On the basis of such findings, would we feel comfortable in talking about a culture, or a subculture, of alcohol? A minority of the rich share many traits of the Sanchez and Rios families, and other families studied by Oscar Lewis—they are

74

alienated from social institutions, tend to be unemployed or irregularly employed, demonstrate high rates of antisocial behavior, and have high divorce rates. Does this small group of the rich constitute a Culture of Affluence?...

Middle Class Myths

The supposed commitment of the middle classes to the virtues of thrift and hard work, to the practices of planning and saving for every painfully-chosen expenditure is, at this point in time, at best a surviving myth reflecting past conditions of dubious prevalence. The middle classes of today are clearly consumption-minded and debt-addicted. So the comparison group against which the poor are judged exists largely as a theoretical category with a theoretical behavior pattern....

No Justification for Poverty

The plain fact is that there is absolutely no justification for the involuntary poverty of a single individual in the United States. This has been true for decades. The instruments needed to produce a material abundance for all are and have been readily available. To convert their potential into reality requires not a vague and politically motivated "unconditional war on poverty," but a class conscious and principled unconditional "war" on capitalism.

"The Myth of Vanishing Poverty," *The People*, March 17, 1984.

Class, according to Weber, Mills and most other observers of the phenomena of social levels, refers to *economic* ranking, to the possession and control of wealth and the sources of wealth, and to relative advantage in the marketplace. *Status,* according to this tripartite view of stratification, is applied to the results of ranking according to prestige and social honor—the esteem that one is able to command; it is reflected primarily in consumption patterns and life style. *Power*—especially as it is perceived in the conglomerate exercise of power known as *party*—means the ability to influence and enforce decisions in community life.

Thus, for example, a millionaire ranks high on the class dimension no matter what his life style may be. In this sense of the term, Howard Hughes, and J. Paul Getty, and Nelson Rockefeller, and Joseph Kennedy are all in the topmost layers of American class structure. The extent to which they are esteemed, the way they live, the influence they exert—all these may be vastly different. But each controls vast wealth and therefore occupies a very high class position. A new-rich Texas oil millionaire ranks right along with old-rich New England descendants of slave-traders and rum-distillers.

75

This is usually not completely true when we look at ranking according to status. On this dimension, those with the old New England slave-and-rum money are way ahead of our Texas oilman. They are expected to attend the charity balls that he is not even invited to. They may live on a street where he is not allowed to buy a house even at a premium. Similarly, even within the same family, the Barnard graduate granddaughter of a Mafia chieftain, with only a fraction of his money (and none of his power), may outrank him socially by quite a few layers.

Power—and party—is based directly on personal and group interests, which may stem from class or status factors, or both, or neither. As an example, what President Eisenhower called the military-industrial complex is, in this sense, a party which exercises great power in American life.

Complex Social Stratification

Class, status and party are, of course, highly correlated but they are by no means identical. Ethnic and racial minorities, for example, rarely achieve a status position commensurate with their class ranking. Political power, particularly at a local level, can be and has been accumulated and exercised by groups of relatively low status and economic class. In American cities, as one example, the police and their allies—what might be termed the "police party"—exercise considerable power in many segments of community life—power far in excess of what one would expect on the basis of class and status factors.

There are a few illustrations of the complexity that underlies the general idea of social stratification, a concept that has appeared deceptively simple to some. To deal with stratification and inequality in American life only, or predominantly, in status terms—to focus in a narrow way on life style, culture, or subculture—is to ignore many of the basic issues involved. Status certainly is almost always the last link in this three-part chain and is dependent on one or both of the other two. To have high prestige in the community, one must have—or one's family or clan must have had at one time—power, or money, or both. To suppose that the road from lower class to middle class position involves changing culture, or life style, or even social acceptability is naive. Inequality in prestige can only be corrected by altering imbalance in wealth and power, seldom by changing table manners or sexual habits.

But this is the basic logic of the culture of poverty cult. Those who are the most devout members of this cult are saying, in effect, that if we can change the culture, the poverty will go away. This is where the inherent logic of this kind of thinking leads.

Perhaps the most fundamental question to ask of those who are enamored of the idea that the poor have one culture and the rich another is to ask, simply, "So what?" Suppose the mythical oil millionaire behaves in an unrefined "lower class" manner, for example. What difference does that make as long as he owns the oil wells? Is the power of the Chairman of the Ways and Means Committee in the state legislature diminished or enhanced in any way by his taste in clothing or music? And suppose every single poor family in America set as its long-range goal that its sons and daughters would get a Ph.D.—who would pay the tuition?

Wealth and Influence

The effect of tastes, child-rearing practices, speech patterns, reading habits, and other cultural factors is relatively small in comparison to the effect of wealth and influence. What I am trying to suggest is that the inclusion in the analytic process of the elements of social stratification that are usually omitted—particularly economic class and power—would produce more significant insights into the circumstances of the poor and the pressures and deprivations with which they live. The simplest—and at the same time, the most significant—proposition in understanding poverty is that it is caused by lack of money. The overwhelming majority of the poor are poor because they have, first: insufficient income; and second: no access to methods of increasing that income—that is, no power. They are too young, too old, too sick; they are bound to the task of caring for small children, or they are simply discriminated against. The facts are clear, and the solution seems rather obvious—raise their income and let their "culture," whatever it might be, take care of itself.

The need to avoid facing this obvious solution—which is very uncomfortable since it requires some substantial changes and redistribution of income—provides the motivation for developing the stabilizing ideology of the culture of poverty which acts to sustain the *status quo* and delay change. The function of the ideology of lower class culture, then, is plainly to maintain inequality in American life.

"The poor choose leisure...because they are paid to do so."

The Poor Can Help Themselves

George Gilder

George Gilder is Program Director of the International Center for Economic Policy Studies and Chairman of the Economic Round-table at the Lehrman Institute. He is the author of *Sexual Suicide, Visible Man,* and *Wealth and Poverty,* which has been nicknamed "the Reaganomics bible." In the following viewpoint, excerpted from that influential work, Mr. Gilder describes what he believes are the three factors that effect poverty: work, family and faith. He states that government intervention in hiring and social programs leads to the breakdown of work and family and therefore encourages poverty.

As you read, consider the following questions:

1. What reasons does Mr. Gilder give for men needing a family in order to be financially productive?
2. Why are women less likely to succeed financially according to Mr. Gilder?
3. According to Mr. Gilder, why are arguments that say minority poverty is caused by discrimination and racism harmful to minority groups?

Living in a world of wealth, the upper classes of Americans have long listened straight-faced and unboggled to the most fantastic tales from the world of the poor. Although inclined to accept Ernest Hemingway's assurances that the rich differ from us chiefly in having more money, we have been willing to suppose that the poor were some alien tribe, exotic in culture and motivation, who can be understood only through the channels of credentialed expertise.

It helped that many of the poor were black. They looked different; perhaps they were different. There came forth a series of authoritative fables: blacks are allegedly matriarchal by nature; like the Irish, the Jews, and other urban immigrants before them, their IQ's were shown to be genetically lower (possibly, in the case of blacks, because of cramped cranial spaces); and they were found to be markedly prone to violent crime and slovenly living. Nonetheless, we could not judge them, it was said by those of liberal spirit, without being guilty of ethnocentrism or cultural imperialism. A propensity for violence, low intelligence, and fatherless homes, it was implied, constitutes a reasonable adaptation to poverty from which we may all learn much.

This attitude, however, required a spirit of cultural relativism so heroic that it could not serve for long, particularly in political formulations. So new approaches emerged, allegedly more enlightened, but with implications equally farfetched. Slavery, discrimination, and deprivation, it was said, have so abused the black psyche that all sorts of new ministrations and therapies are needed to redeem it; racism and unemployment still inflict such liabilities that vast new programs of public employment and affirmative action are required to overcome them. The reasonable inference arises that even though blacks are not genetically inferior, science proves them to be so damaged by racism and poverty that they are inferior now.

Not only do these notions cause serious strain to the spirit of liberalism when confronting specific specimens of this maimed but deserving race, but such attitudes also perpetuate the idea that the poor, for whatever reason, are still very different from us. This belief permits a series of new fables to arise, some explicit, most implicit in government programs.

The Lust for Labor

For example, most of us work for money and enjoy leisure. The poor, it is implied, despite their generally more onerous jobs, do not. They so lust for labor, so they tell all inquiring scholars, that their willingness to work is unaffected by levels of welfare and in-kind support substantially higher than the available wage; they even clamor to enter the work force in the face of effective tax rates on work (through reductions in welfare payments) of nearly 100 percent.

All American ethnic groups in the past rose out of poverty partly by learning English and downplaying their own languages. The current foreign poor, mostly Hispanic, are thought to require instruction chiefly in their native tongue, for reasons of ethnic pride.

Middle-class Americans are demonstrably devastated by divorce and separation: they leave their jobs, income plummets, health deteriorates; they drink and philander; their children behave badly in school. But the poor and their children are assumed to be relatively unshaken by a plague of family breakdowns; at least any resulting lower income and employment levels are said to be due to discrimination, and the behavior of the children is regarded to be little influenced by the absence of fathers.

Most American men earn more money than their wives; men that don't tend to leave, or be left, in large numbers. Yet poor men are assumed to be unaffected by the higher relative incomes available to their wives from welfare and affirmative action, which are alleged to have no relationship to high rates of unemployment and illegitimacy.

People Conversion

If we have a specialty in this country, it's people-conversion. We convert poor, ignorant, peasant people into high-class well-to-do people. Those poor peasant Irish, Chinese, Japanese, Jewish and many ex-slaves, in the space of less than a century, have been converted into middle-class, two-television, two-car, eating-plenty-of-food (usually too much) families. The difference between today's poor and yesterday's is that yesterday's poor had open economic opportunities for upward mobility. Today's poor have opportunities stifled, or eliminated, with welfare put in its place. It's a shame nobody sees the big picture—and its hopelessness.

Walter E. Williams, "The Hopelessness of The Welfare Mentality," The Heritage Features Syndicate, 1982.

Perhaps most important of all, every successful ethnic group in our history rose up by working harder than other classes, low-paid jobs, with a vanguard of men in entrepreneurial roles. But the current poor, so it is supposed, can leapfrog drudgery by education and credentials, or be led as a group from poverty, perhaps by welfare mothers trained for government jobs. These views depict the current poor as a race so alien to the entire American experience, so radically different in motive and character from whites, that one can speak in terms of a new form of bigotry.

The notion of liberal racism is perhaps needlessly provacative. Liberals are not racists any more than all but a small, dwindling, and utterly uninfluential minority of other Americans are. But the response of the dominantly liberal media to the racial situation is so quixotic and peculiar as to be reprehensible in its own special way. For example, anyone who has spent any time at all among the American political and economic elite knows that it is desperately eager to appoint blacks to high positions whenever they are reasonably able to perform the duties. The more prestigious American universities avidly pursue black Ph.D.'s and pay them on average some two thousand dollars more than white professors with similar credentials and experience. Yet every American newspaper and magazine treated the appointment of Franklin Thomas as head of the Ford Foundation as if it were some amazing triumph, a startling breakthrough, although Thomas had previously turned down a post in the U.S. cabinet, had already served as a temporary chief of the Whitney Foundation, professed the same impeccably fashionable views as his predecessor, McGeorge Bundy, and was chosen with the highest possible enthusiasm by the board....

Refusal to Tell the Truth

The refusal of American leaders to tell the truth about blacks is more important when it comes to black poverty. The prevailing expressed opinion is that racism and discrimination still explain the low incomes of blacks. This proposition is at once false and invidious. Not only does it slander white Americans, it deceives and demoralizes blacks. Not only does it obstruct the truth, it encourages, by its essential incredibility, the alternate falsehood, held in private by many blacks and whites, that blacks cannot now make it in America without vast federal assistance, without, indeed, the very government programs that in fact account for the worst aspects of black poverty and promise to perpetuate it. Finally, the liberal belief in bigotry as an explanation for the condition of blacks leads to still more preposterous theories about the alleged poverty of other groups, from women to Hispanics, and to a generally manic-depressive vision of the economy, in which poverty is seen both as more extreme and more remediable than it is.

The first thing to understand is that regardless of the affluence of the American economy, we live in a world full of poor people. Modern transport and communications ensure that increasing numbers will be both eager and able to reach our shores. Unless we wish to adopt an immoral and economically self-destructive policy of prohibiting immigration, there will be poverty in America for centuries to come. The policies and approaches we have adopted in our neurotic concern about blacks will likely be applied to many millions of others. The potential injury that could be inflicted on our economy and on the poor people in it is quite incalculable. But, on the basis of the long and thoroughly unambiguous experience of our government in blighting the lives of blacks and Indians, one can only predict that the damage will be

81

tragically great.

The only dependable route from poverty is always work, family, and faith. The first principle is that in order to move up, the poor must not only work, they must work harder than the classes above them. Every previous generation of the lower class has made such efforts. But the current poor, white even more than black, are refusing to work hard. Irwin Garfinkel and Robert Haveman, authors of an ingenious and sophisticated study of what they call *Earnings Capacity Utilization Rates*, have calculated the degree to which various income groups use their opportunities—how hard they work outside the home. This study shows that, for several understandable reasons, the current poor work substantially less, for fewer hours and weeks a year, and earn less in proportion to their age, education, and other credentials (even *after* correcting the figures for unemployment, disability, and presumed discrimination) than either their predecessors in American cities or those now above them on the income scale. (The study was made at the federally funded Institute for Research on Poverty at the University of Wisconsin and used data from the census and the Michigan longitudinal survey.) The findings lend important confirmation to the growing body of evidence that work effort is the crucial unmeasured variable in American productivity and income distribution, and that current welfare and other subsidy programs substantially reduce work. The poor choose leisure not because of moral weakness, but because they are paid to do so.

Work, Family and Faith

A program to lift by transfers and preferences the incomes of less diligent groups is politically divisive—and very unlikely—because it incurs the bitter resistance of the real working class. In addition, such an effort breaks the psychological link between effort and reward, which is crucial to long-run upward mobility. Because effective work consists not in merely fulfilling the requirements of labor contracts, but in "putting out" with alertness and emotional commitment, workers have to understand and feel deeply that what they are given depends on what they give—that they must supply work in order to demand goods. Parents and schools must inculcate this idea in their children both by instruction and example. Nothing is more deadly to achievement than the belief that effort will not be rewarded, that the world is a bleak and discriminatory place in which only the predatory and the specially preferred can get ahead. Such a view in the home discourages the work effort in school that shapes earnings capacity afterward. As with so many aspects of human performance, work effort begins in family experiences, and its sources can be best explored through an examination of family structure.

Indeed, after work the second principle of upward mobility is the maintenance of monogramous marriage and family. Adjusting for discrimination against women and for child-care responsibilities, the Wisconsin study indicates that married men work between two and one-third and four times harder than married women, and more than twice as hard as female family heads. The work effort of married men increases with their age, credentials, education, job experience, and birth of children, while the work effort of married women steadily declines. Most important in judging the impact of marriage, husbands, work 50 percent harder than bachelors of comparable age, education, and skills.

The Effects of Marriage

The effect of marriage, thus, is to increase the work effort of men by about half. Since men have higher earnings capacity to begin with, and since the female capacity-utilization figures would be even lower without an adjustment for discrimination, it is manifest that the maintenance of families is the key factor in reducing poverty.

Once a family is headed by a woman, it is almost impossible for it to greatly raise its income even if the woman is highly educated and trained and she hires day-care or domestic help. Her family responsibilities and distractions tend to prevent her from the kind of all-out commitment that is necessary for the full use of earning power. Few women with children make earning money the top priority in their lives.

A married man, on the other hand, is spurred by the claims of family to channel his otherwise disruptive male aggressions into his performance as a provider for a wife and children. These sexual differences alone, which manifest themselves in all societies known to anthropology, dictate that the first priority of any serious program against poverty is to strengthen the male role in poor families....

Disciplined Sexuality

The short-sighted outlook of poverty stems largely from the breakdown of family responsibilities among fathers. The lives of the poor, all too often, are governed by the rhythms of tension and release that characterize the sexual experience of young single men. Because female sexuality, as it evolved over the millennia, is psychologically rooted in the bearing and nurturing of children, women have long horizons whithin their very bodies, glimpses of eternity within their wombs. Civilized society is dependent upon the submission of the short-term sexuality of young men to the extended maternal horizons of women. This is what happens in monogamous marriage; the man disciplines his sexuality and extends it into the future through the womb of a woman. The

83

woman gives him access to his children, otherwise forever denied him; and he gives her the product of his labor, otherwise dissipated on temporary pleasures. The woman gives him a unique link to the future and a vision of it; he gives her faithfulness and a commitment to a lifetime of hard work. If work effort is the first principle of overcoming poverty, marriage is the prime source of upwardly mobile work.

It is love that changes the short horizons of youth and poverty into the long horizons of marriage and career. When marriages fail, the man often returns to the more primitive rhythms of singleness. On the average, his income drops by one-third and he shows a far higher propensity for drink, drugs, and crime. But when marriages in general hold firm and men in general love and support their children, Banfield's lower-class style changes into middle-class futurity.

The Rewards of Not Working

If we do not decrease the rewards for not working, there will continue to be a decreasing participation rate, falling productivity, and declining real wages. Poverty will increase because people do what they are rewarded for doing. As long as poverty pays well, the number in poverty but for the various "income security" programs will continue to grow and our affluence will continue to decline. It is that slide into the abyss that Reagan has worked hard to reverse by developing proposals for changes in government programs that, if instituted, will turn the country around.

Yale Brozen, "Government and the Rich," *National Review,* July 9, 1982.

The key to the intractable poverty of the hardcore American poor is the dominance of single and separated men in poor communities. Black "unrelated individuals" are not much more likely to be in poverty than white ones. The problem is neither race nor matriarchy in any meaningful sense. It is familial anarchy among the concentrated poor of the inner city, in which flamboyant and impulsive youths rather than responsible men provide the themes of aspiration. The result is that male sexual rhythms tend to prevail, and boys are brought up without authoritative fathers in the home to instill in them the values of responsible paternity: the discipline and love of children and the dependable performance of the provider role. "If she wants me *she'll* pay," one young stud assured me in prison, and perhaps, in the welfare culture, she can and will. Thus the pattern is extended into future generations....

An analysis of poverty that begins and ends with family structure and marital status would explain far more about the problem than most of the distributions of income, inequality, unemployment, education, IQ, race, sex, home ownership, location, discrimination, and all the other items usually multiply regressed and correlated on academic computers. But even an analysis of work and family would miss what is perhaps the most important of the principles of upward mobility under capitalism—namely, faith....

Faith in man, faith in the future, faith in the rising returns of giving, faith in the mutual benefits of trade, faith in the providence of God are all essential to successful capitalism. All are necessary to sustain the spirit of work and enterprise against the setbacks and frustrations it inevitably meets in a fallen world; to inspire trust and cooperation in an economy where they will often be betrayed; to encourage the foregoing of present pleasures in the name of a future that may well go up in smoke; to promote risk and initiative in a world where the rewards all vanish unless others join the game. In order to give without the certainty of future value, in order to work beyond the requirement of the job, one has to have confidence in a higher morality: a law of compensations beyond the immediate and distracting struggles of existence.

Faith, in all its multifarious forms and luminosities, can by itself move the mountains of sloth and depression that afflict the world's stagnant economies; it brought immigrants thousands of miles and with pennies in their pockets to launch the American empire of commerce; and it performs miracles daily in our present impasse.

In general, however, upward mobility depends on all three principles—work, family, and faith—interdependently reaching toward children and future. These are the pillars of a free economy and a prosperous society. They are being eroded now in America by the intellectual and political leaders of perhaps the freest and most prosperous of all the world's societies.

"The poor had better be there to be
championed....Any suggestion that the lot of them
has been improved meets with great scorn."

Poverty Exists in America

Meg Greenfield

Meg Greenfield received her B.A. from Smith College and attended
Cambridge University in England as a Fulbright Scholar. The re-
cipient of numerous journalism awards, including the Pulitzer
Prize in 1978, Ms. Greenfield is currently the editorial page editor
of the *Washington Post.* She is probably best known for her bi-
monthly editorial column in *Newsweek* magazine. Meg Greenfield
received a Pulitzer Prize in 1978 for editorial writing in recognition of her newspaper work. In the following viewpoint, she
claims that most Americans erroneously believe that poverty is a
self-perpetuated state. She denies this and contends that the poor
can be uplifted by a compassionate society and that Americans
should stop waging a silent war against them.

As you read, consider the following questions:

1. What is wrong, according to the author, with the term "true
   need"?
2. According to the author, why are people who believe the
   poor can overcome economic hardship unfair?
3. Does Ms. Greenfield believe public aid is justified?

The trouble begins with the term "true need." It is condescending, unpersuaded, vaguely "Oh, yeah? Show me"—a term that tends to push a supplicant to the wall. "True need" suspects a hoax or at least a deplorable want of effort. So you can only qualify for the government-provided blessings that flow from proof of this condition with some corresponding loss of dignity; here, look for yourself at the mess that is my (family, body, life). Inspect the kitchen, the bedroom, the medical records, the receipts. I just can't do it by myself—honest.

Before we had "true need" and the "truly needy," we had "poverty" and "the poor." I remember thinking, in the mid-1960s when these became operative words, how refreshingly simple, direct, respectable, even classic they were. No more "disadvantaged," "underprivileged" and the rest of that disgusting bureaucratic pack. "Poverty"—right out of the Bible and Piers Plowman; it said what it meant.

And yet, it seems to me that in recent times there has been a change for the worse in the way this term is employed, too. "Poverty"—its very down-through-the-centuries quality lends a connotation of permanence and hopelessness to it as a condition. "You have the poor always with you" is the idea, but at first this was invoked only by right-wing antagonists of the Johnson Administration's effort to fight poverty. Now I sense a comparable belief in some quarters on the other side. It suits their new opposition politics and their self-image as affluent champions of the poor: the poor had better always be there to be championed. Any suggestion, in fact, that the lot of any of them has been improved meets with great scorn.

There's Money In Poverty

Unfortunately, much of the sound, sensible protest against this and the agitation for a more reliable system of aiding the poor are overshadowed by dilettantes on the other side—Beautiful People liberals and some who ply that tax-exempt, eminently deductible and free-food-at-the-conference life that goes with ministering bureaucratically to the poor. I can't remember who said, apropos of this burgeoning industry, that "there's money in poverty," but he was right.

Still, in some of their distracting argument you sense more than that: you sense self-satisfaction, moral pretentiousness, a club to beat the opponents with, a different kind of justification for one's privilege from that called forth by the conservative right. It's enough, in these circles, to bleed for the poor (whoever they may be); you surely don't have to become one of them. So the poor remain a useful abstraction, attractive and imposed-upon victims in the aggregate, except when they insist on such disruptive practices as praying publicly or displayinig some racial prejudice, whereupon they become some other much-denounced group.

Will you permit me to reach in here right now and fish Bill Moyers out of any suspicion of being part of this group? I don't think he belongs there. I think there is, given the character of the awful argument, a positive need for journalistic exploration of what is or isn't going on among poor people in America. And I guess I should also provide the self-evident reservation: far from all Reaganites or liberal celebrities or do-gooders or rugged individualists or medianiks fall into these categories. But too many do, and I think the argument over the condition of the nation's poor people now going on has taken on its infuriating, aimless quality precisely because the positions put forward by these people are so self-interested, so self-indulgent, so suspect.

Hurting The Poor

Surely at a minimum this much can be conceded on the one side: government *has* become too big and meddlesome. There *has* been extravagance and cheating on social programs that could be curbed. Inflation *was* a killer of the poor. And on the other, this needs to be conceded: the Reagan program *is* hurting very poor people. Public aid *is* justified and necessary to help them, all of them. This should *not* be made contingent upon degradation to a condition of desperation. It should be automatic. We are the richest country on earth.

Other advanced countries have real safety nets and programs

that go into effect to protect the health and well-being of citizens faced with either sudden or chronic adversity. It is incredible that we should have to be trotting out our most hard-luck citizens and saying, "Step right up to the camera, little lady; show them your scars."

The War About Poverty

What we are having in the 1980s, in other words, is not a war against poverty, but rather a war about poverty.

Who are the participants in this war? Practically all of us who are not poor, so far as I can see. But some, alas, are much more active combatants than others. And they are identifiable by their philosophical predilections. For one side, almost parodied by some of the dandied-up-conservative rich, Ben Franklin (as distinct from Che Guevara) is the founding authority. There's not a one of his complacent little maxims that doesn't seem to them applicable to those currently in need.

A long line of American politicians has been a part of this tradition. They are the ones who, viewing the bleakest social landscape the South Bronx or Appalachia has to offer, invariably are moved to recall their own early deprivations and subsequent success, offering this up as a useful inspiration to their sullen audience. The message is, variously: what a wonderful country we live in; see, if you would just work a little harder you could do it; I got mine, you get yours.

All this rests on some mythic assumptions of classlessness, of a wholly benign economic environment in which one racial or ethnic or economic or professional group never owes its good fortune to the miseries of another, of a kind of simple, linear upward mobility available to anyone who sets out to achieve it. Good-news stories are taken as the norm. God bless you, Tiny Tim.

For such people there can be no built-in predicament or situation that could hold back anyone. And certainly there cannot be a large amount of economic hardship requiring the governmental equivalent of the doctor's heroic measures. To believe otherwise would be unbearable. As it is, however, the assumptions are seen as justifying not only great economic disparities, but also a kind of weird pep-rally pride. You too, the losers and the lost are informed, could one day be at the top of the heap.

"You have only to drive down any main street...to know that the official figure that one in every 7 or so Americans is living in poverty does not reflect the physical reality."

Poverty in America Is Exaggerated

By Howard Banks and Jayne A. Pearl

Howard Banks left the aircraft industry after 10 years to pursue a career in journalism. In 1970 he joined the staff of the London-based *The Economist* and became industrial editor, aviator specialist, and their first west coast correspondent. Mr. Banks is now bureau chief and associate editor in Washington, DC for *Forbes* magazine. He is the author of *The Rise and Fall of Freddie Laker.* Jayne Pearl studied journalism at Hofstra University in New York and is working on a degree in economics. She has been a reporter for *Forbes* for four years and works in the Washington bureau. In the following viewpoint, Howard Banks and Jayne A. Pearl question recent poverty statistics and conclude that poverty is not epidemic. The so-called poor have televisions, portable stereos, and enough food.

As you read, consider the following questions:

1. What is wrong with poverty statistics, according to the authors?
2. Do the authors believe that malnutrition exists in America?
3. Why are welfare payments "the key to people staying poor," according to the authors?

Howard Banks and Jayne A. Pearl, "Poverty in America." Reprinted by permission of *Forbes* magazine, August 29, 1983. © Forbes Inc., 1983.

A good section of the American population and most of the media have been on a guilt trip ever since statistics from the Census Bureau showed that 34.4 million Americans, 15% of the population, are now considered to be below the poverty line, up from 14% in 1981. The implications seemed clear: Reagan's policies have helped the rich and hurt the poor. Far from questioning the statistics, the Administration responded immediately with a hunger task force. No one seemed willing to challenge the poverty figures. Certainly not the liberals who profess to believe that pouring money on the disadvantaged solves the problem; nor the conservatives, embarrassed at what they expect would be thought bad taste if they challenged the figures.

All this and natural compassion makes judicious analysis of the poverty statistics difficult. And yet, since poverty is the kind of issue that decides elections and the fates of governments, honest analysis is essential to the survival of democracy.

Poverty Statistics Grossly Inaccurate

A major problem is with the poverty statistics themselves. "They are probably the worst federal statistics ever developed," says Robert B. Carleson, special assistant to the President for policy development. The official poverty level was first set in 1961 when the Social Security Administration devised an economy food plan with the Agriculture Department, set at the cost of a minimum adequate diet. On the assumption that a family spends one-third of its income on food, this figure was then multiplied by three. Since then it has been adjusted only to cover inflation, but using the standard Consumer Price Index, which is essentially middle-class based. The CPI overcounts things like mortgage interest rate changes, which do not affect the poor, and undercounts utilities, which are a major burden for those low-incomes....

In theoretical terms, the poverty statistics are thought to be pretty good. They are collected through monthly Labor Force interviews for the Current Population Survey, where 61,500 households are interviewed. Every March a supplemental interview is included, some by phone, some in person. The 1,500 interviewers are said to be among the best-trained in America. Each household in the survey is interviewed for four months and, after an eight-month gap, for four more months.

Secrecy about Income

Of course, a cynic would ask: Are the respondents being totally frank about their other income? If your choice was to be scrupulously honest and lose your food stamps, what would you do if the chance of being found out was minimal? An elderly lady was asked what she would do if her few hundred shares of AT&T went up and disqualified her for the subsidized housing she occupies. "I just won't tell them," she answered honestly.

There is also the matter of the underground economy, where those able to get some kind of part-time work forget to mention it. How about Simone, a graduate student at a Texas university with a teaching income of $5,500 plus a secretarial income of $3,000, which she did not report. "It bothers me that I don't report it," she says, "but I figured it would cost me $400." An upstate New York builder tells of laying off two men on Wednesday. On Friday they registered for unemployment insurance. On Monday they went to work for another builder. Off the books, of course. Manhattan taxi drivers are notoriously casual about reporting their earnings to the IRS. A good many of them presumably figure in the poverty figures.

Poverty Statistics Exaggerated

What is poverty? You only have to drive down any main street, or into the depths of the countryside, to know that the official figure that one in every seven or so Americans is living in poverty does not reflect the physical reality. Nowhere can you find starving masses, endemic malnutrition. Of course there are poor people, living in substandard housing where there are rats and roaches, where the windows have been broken and not fixed. Where the mailboxes have been hammered open by welfare-check thieves. Where the kids wear hand-me-down clothes that are sometimes not warm enough in winter. Where heating and air-conditioning are bad or nonexistent. Where a window fan is the height of luxury.

Poverty Facts Vs. Complaints

Does hunger mean famine and starvation? Children with swollen bellies and sunken eyes still exist in less fortunate nations, but not in the United States. The presence of that kind of hunger is not nearly as prevalent as the people who complain about it.

Becci M. Breining, *USA Today,* April 2, 1984.

But they are not suffering in the way that the geniunely poverty-stricken do in the slums of Calcutta or Rio. Even in the worst block that one *Forbes* reporter could find in a black Washington, D.C. neighborhood (the cops made him report back that he had gotten out all right), nearly everybody had a television set, some color. Radios are everywhere, the kids are carrying portable stereos, cruelly dubbed Third World briefcases. Many families have cars, though most are early 1970s gas-guzzlers available cheap on the third-hand market. And telephones are standard, though that is changing as installation and monthly rentals rise.

Hunger is subjective, but malnutrition is a matter that can be assesed medically. "There's never been a real case made that there is any endemic malnutrition in this country," says George Graham, professor of human nutrition and pediatrics at Johns Hopkins University. And he includes all the work in the late 1960s that led to the explosion of the food programs intended to aid the poor, including those started by President Lyndon Johnson. People claim there is evidence of stunting in some populations, he says. But the black are, on average, taller for their age and the Hispanics and Orientals shorter, yet Orientals academically outperform all, including whites. The economist, Walter Williams, of George Mason University, expects the President's task force on hunger will find little remaining malnutrition in America. Either it will involve the elderly with no, or a neglectful, family. Or it will be seen to be self-imposed. "Unwise management," he says. "Parents who give their kids Coca-Cola and potato chips for breakfast." History provides the best lesson on how to deal with poverty in a rich and evolving society such as the U.S. Throwing government money at the problem is not what the lesson teaches. As Walter Williams points out, capitalism and the economic growth it stimulated raised the American working class to middle-class affluence. "A rapidly growing economy solves many social ills," he says. To the extent, then, that taxes to pay for transfer payments inhibit recovery, they may be hurting the very people for whose benefit the taxes are being levied.

Room for Cynicism

In the 1950s no less than 30% of the population was believed to be below the poverty line. But that had declined by a third in the early 1960s when the serious counting began. Look at the chart showing the decline, and you will find that it began to level out at around 10% to 12% in the late 1960s. That refusal of the poverty proportion to decline, coincidentally, came after the big push to provide aid for the poor. There's room for cynicism here, but even more room for questioning those ultraexpensive antipoverty programs. There seems to be a floor level of around 10% below which official poverty refuses to decline.

The unpalatable conclusion is that the whole system of aid through payments and aid in kind is the key to people staying poor. No, that is not saying that people are cheating. Just that the poor are reacting to economic stimulus in the same way a commodity dealer does when told that the Florida orange harvest has been devastated by frost: each acts in his or her own best economic interest.

Williams says: "The poor are poor, not stupid. If you give them incentives to be poor they will stay that way. Entitlements subsidize poverty and anyone knows that when you subsidize something you get more of it and when you tax something you get less."

Throwing checks at a serious and fundamental social problem makes people believe they are doing something and has created two constituent groups anxious to keep the money flowing: those that receive, and those that earn their living doling it out.

The Imprisoned Bourgeosis

Imprisoned inside every poor person is a clean-living bourgeois yearning to break free. This is the tacit assumption of social work, public and private; often it proves true (if it didn't there would be no such thing as upward mobility). But often it proves false. There are people living in degraded circumstances who are incapable of living otherwise: destructive, self-destructive, incompetent.

"The Undeserving Poor," *The National Review,* March 4, 1983.

Both the definitions and the statistics about poverty in America are highly suspect. But even worse are the political conclusions some people try to draw from them. At least as good a case can be made that the Reagan policies are good for the poor as that they hurt the poor.

Recognizing Statements That Are Provable

From various sources of information we are constantly confronted with statements and generalizations about social and moral problems. In order to think clearly about these problems, it is useful if one can make a basic distinction between statements for which evidence can be found and other statements which cannot be verified or proved because evidence is not available, or the issue is so controversial that it cannot be definitely proved.

Readers should constantly be aware that magazines, newspapers, and other sources often contain statements of a controversial nature. The following activity is designed to allow experimentation with statements that are provable and those that are not.

Most of the following statements are taken from the viewpoints in this chapter. Consider each statement carefully. *Mark P for any statement you believe is provable. Mark U for any statement you feel is unprovable because of the lack of evidence. Mark C for statements you think are too controversial to be proved to everyone's satisfaction.*

If you are doing this activity as a member of a class or group, compare your answers with those of other class or group members. Be able to defend your answers. You may discover that others will come to different conclusions than you. Listening to the reasons others present for their answers may give you valuable insights in recognizing statements that are provable.

If you are reading this book alone, ask others if they agree with your answers. You too will find this interaction very valuable.

P = *provable*
U = *unprovable*
C = *too controversial*

1. That the poor in America constitute a separate culture is a manifest absurdity.

2. The poor are different in significant ways from the rest of us and these differences are cultural.

3. Inequality in prestige can only be corrected by altering imbalance in wealth and power, seldom by changing table manners or sexual habits.

4. All American ethnic groups in the past rose out of poverty partly by learning English and downplaying their own languages.

5. Few women with children make earning money the top priority in their lives.

6. The poor choose leisure because they are paid to do so.

7. Not only have high-income persons not benefited disproportionately from tax cuts, but the gross amounts they are paying are greater than before the cuts went into effect.

8. Today, poverty seems not on the way to being eliminated but rather to be growing.

9. Many Americans are unable to work—even if jobs were available—because they are too old, too sick, or taking care of children.

10. In the United States, five hundred corporations control over 80 percent of all industrial assets.

11. Only a free market is consistent with political liberty.

12. You have the poor always with you.

13. Government has become too big and meddlesome.

14. Inflation is a killer of the poor.

15. The official poverty level was first set in 1961 by the Social Security Administration and the Agriculture Department.

16. In the United States, nowhere can you find starving masses and endemic malnutrition.

17. Both the definitions and the statistics about poverty in America are highly suspect.

Periodical Bibliography

The following list of periodical articles deals with the subject matter of this chapter.

Christine Adamec "Confessions Of A Welfare Worker," *Conservative Digest,* February 1984.

Jonathon Alter, Alexander Stille, and others "Homeless in America," *Newsweek,* January 2, 1984.

Howard Baetjer Jr. "Does Welfare Diminish Poverty?" *The Freeman,* April 1984.

James Bovard "How Many Federal Programs Are Needed to Cure Hunger in America?" *Conservative Digest,* February 1984.

William F. Buckley Jr. "The Poor Get Poorer," *National Review,* April 30, 1982.

Alexis Gelber and others "The Welfare Crisis," *Newsweek,* July 25, 1983.

Nick Kotz "The Politics of Hunger," *New Republic,* April 30, 1984.

Kate Leishman "Trials of Two Welfare States," *The Atlantic Monthly,* November 1983.

Richard McGahey "The 'Underclass' Label and Social Policy," *USA Today,* September 1983.

Lawrence Maloney, Jeannye Thornton "No Way Out," *U.S. News and World Report,* July 16, 1982.

Daniel Patrick Moynihan "One-Third of a Nation," *New Republic,* June 9, 1982.

New Republic "Banquets and Breadlines," January 9 and 16, 1984.

Cesar Perales "Myths About Poverty," *New York Times,* October 21, 1983.

Michael Radding "Street People," *America,* February 18, 1984.

Alvin Schorr "Redefining Poverty Levels," *New York Times,* May 9, 1984.

Beth Spring "Is There Hunger in America?" *Christianity Today,* March 16, 1984.

Is the US Fair to Immigrants?

"Allowing uncontrolled immigration to deprive our own disadvantaged of desperately needed economic opportunities is...unreasonable and unjust."

Illegal Immigration Should Be Stopped

Federation for American Immigration Reform

The Federation for American Immigration Reform (FAIR) is a national, nonprofit organization whose goals are to end illegal immigration into the United States and to set a limit on total legal immigration. In the following viewpoint, FAIR states its position that the tide of illegal immigration seriously harms U.S. workers and illegal immigrants themselves, who are often exploited and enslaved by unscrupulous employers.

As you read, consider the following questions:

1. Why do employers prefer to hire illegal immigrants, according to FAIR?
2. What are the "seven facts" presented to support the thesis that immigration is "uncontrolled"?
3. According to FAIR, who benefits from illegal immigration?

John Tanton, from a direct mail letter published by FAIR, The Federation for American Immigration Reform, 2028 P Street NW, Washington, DC, 20036. Reprinted with permission.

Immigrants helped build this country. But unchecked illegal immigration poses a clear and present danger to our own disadvantaged.

For the future well-being not only of Americans but also those living in underdeveloped nations, this problem must not be ignored. For the preservation of the basic ideas and values of American life, I believe the solution must come from people of compassion and foresight....

Illegal Immigration Hurts Americans

Disadvantaged Americans pay a particularly heavy price for illegal immigration. Millions of illegal workers compete with minorities, youth, and women for scarce jobs.

Many employers seem to prefer to hire illegal immigrants because they can be more easily exploited than American workers. As just one example, FAIR's office received a call from a seamstress whose boss asked her to train a new employee, an illegal immigrant. Our caller was black, she was poor, and, as soon as she finished training the illegal worker, she was fired.

In Congressional testimony, former National Urban League President Vernon Jordan indicated that illegal immigration "makes it tougher for citizens to find jobs or to demand decent working conditions."

Some people argue that these illegal immigrants are only taking hard, dirty jobs that Americans are unwilling to do. The truth is that Americans already make up the majority of workers in *all* these low-paying occupations. And the presence of illegal immigrants makes the exploitation of our own American workers much easier.

Allowing uncontrolled immigration to deprive our own disadvantaged of desperately needed economic opportunities is not only unreasonable and unjust, but it has also aggravated ethnic and racial tensions to the point of violence in parts of the country. In Chicago, shooting incidents erupted between Mexican-Americans and illegal Mexican immigrants competing with each other for work and housing. The *Washington Post* cited the influx of Cuban and Haitian refugees as one of the causes of the Miami Liberty City riots. Flare-ups of violence have also occurred in Colorado, Texas and Kansas.

As long as our decision-makers in government continue to turn a blind eye to this problem, we face a growing risk of an uncontrollable backlash against immigrants and refugees that could destroy all hope of achieving a humane and rational U.S. policy on immigration.

Uncontrolled immigration also poses dangers that seriously threaten not only America's poor, but *all* Americans as well.

Net immigration now accounts for *50 percent* of the annual U.S. population growth. While Americans are sacrificing to have

smaller families, continued immigration at current levels—800,000 legal immigrants in 1980 and perhaps an even higher number of illegal immigrants—will add more than 70,000,000 people to the U.S. population in just 50 years, with no end in sight.

Every addition to our population adds significantly to our needs for rapidly diminishing natural resources, and thus adds to the pressures to exploit and destroy our natural heritage.

Most people agree that more must be done to conserve energy. But what we managed to save by the 55 mph speed limit has been offset by the additional demands of just two years' influx of immigrants. The immigrants who arrived in the last decade alone use half the oil production of the Alaska Pipeline!

Uncontrolled Immigration

"Uncontrolled" is indeed the word to describe the results of current U.S. immigration policy. Consider these facts:

1. Estimates of the number of illegal immigrants in the United States range from 3.5 to 12 million, but government officials admit that they have no idea how many are in the country.

2. Over the past four years the Immigration and Naturalization Service has apprehended one million people a year attempting to enter the U.S. illegally, ten times the number in 1965. And a report by the Select Committee on Population to the U.S. House of Representatives estimates that between *2 to 3 times* that many

illegal aliens were able to enter the United States successfully.

3. Immigration to the United States is at record levels. In 1980, the U.S. took twice as many legal immigrants and refugees as the rest of the world combined. Almost 20 percent of all the immigrants who have come to this country in our history came in the last decade alone.

4. Jobs are the magnet which attract illegal immigrants, yet it is not against the law to hire an illegal—although it is against the law for an illegal immigrant to take a job in this country.

5. Immigration and Naturalization Service figures show that, in 1978, 15 percent of the 9.3 million visitors to the United States were not known to have left.

6. A widespread black market in student visas exists. In January 1980, the *New York Times* reported that black market student visa forms signed by U.S. college officials were on sale for $700 to $1500 on the black market in Iran.

Illegals Steal American Jobs

In his testimony before the Senate Judiciary Committee's Subcommittee on Immigration and Refugee Policy, Attorney General Smith stated that today only 15 percent of illegal aliens work as farm laborers, while 30 percent hold blue collar industrial jobs. There are millions of unemployed Americans who do want to work, and who would love to have jobs held by illegal aliens.

According to a December 1978 Congressional Budget Office report, every unemployed American costs the taxpayers $7,000 per year in unemployment benefits, food stamps and other payments. That is $7 billion for every million unemployed Americans. Both Labor Department and INS officials have repeatedly stated that illegal aliens in the American workforce are a major cause of high unemployment.

Palmer Stacy, "Uncontrolled Immigration: Silent Threat to America," *Human Events*, December 12, 1981.

---

7. If illegal immigrants were not taking so many jobs in America, unemployment could be brought under 4 percent, according to former Secretary of Labor Ray Marshall.

The United States has virtually relinquished its right to determine who will or will not live here. This surrender is not only a threat to the well-being of every American, but it holds devastating consequences for countless numbers in poor countries.

Underdeveloped Countries Are Harmed

Many who favor unlimited, unrestricted immigration to the United States are sincere humanitarians. They focus their concerns on the comparatively small number who manage to emigrate to the United States. But what of the plight of the millions of unseen countrymen left behind to live with conditions that the emigrants might have helped to change?

Open immigration policies in the U.S. contribute significantly to what the *Christian Science Monitor* has called the "brain, brawn, and gumption drain" of less developed countries. Contrary to popular belief, it is not the destitute who emigrate. More often it is the energetic, the talented, the skilled and the educated who have the means and the initiative to leave their native lands.

With the United States acting as a "safety valve," the elites in these nations are able to avoid seeking solutions to their problems of underdevelopment and overpopulation. The result is continuing poverty, misery, and hopelessness for the masses of people who will never be able to emigrate.

In a Pulitzer-Prize-winning study, the *Des Moines Register-Guard* found that for every person added to our population, 1.5 acres of prime agricultural land goes out of production to make way for new houses, roads, and shopping centers. If growth rates continue, the U.S. will cease to be an exporter of food shortly after the year 2000. What will it profit the hungry people of the world if our growing population forces us to stop exporting food?

Does *anyone* benefit from the rising tide of illegal immigration? Business interests that employ illegals at low wages benefit. Many illegals are better off financially here than in their own countries. But many others are ruthlessly exploited by unscrupulous employers and held in virtual servitude, denied the rights and privileges we want to be able to extend to everyone who lives in the United States within the law.

"[Illegal] immigration is a large plus for this country, a development we should be cheering, not deploring."

Illegal Immigration Should Be Allowed

Lou Cannon

Lou Cannon is the White House Correspondent for the *Washington Post.* In 1982 he authored *Reagan* "the definitive biography" of Ronald Reagan. Cannon's previous books are *Ronnie and Jesse: A Political Odyssey* and *Reporting: An Inside View.* In the following viewpoint, Mr. Cannon explains why, "far from ripping off the system, illegal aliens are more likely to be subsidizing it." He believes that measures to seal off our border would be unfair to illegal immigrants and to US citizens.

As you read, consider the following questions:

1. How, according to Mr. Cannon, do illegal immigrants economically benefit the U.S.?
2. How does illegal immigration benefit U.S. agriculture, according to the author?
3. Why, according to the author, do illegal aliens not affect U.S. employment?

Lou Cannon, "Mexican Illegals Are Beneficial to US," *The Minneapolis Star*, August 13, 1979. © The Washington Post.

Along the dusty Mexican border in California and Texas, new chain-link fences are being built to keep out unwanted immigrants. In Sacramento the California Legislature looks with suspicion at the bilingual education it once pioneered. In Los Angeles there is renewed political pressure to deny non-emergency medical services to county patients unable to provide evidence of citizenship.

These reactions reflect a persistent and growing belief that Mexican immigrants, especially illegal *indocumentados*, are a drain on tax-supported services, with the high-fertility potential of turning southern California into a Spanish-speaking version of Quebec. Often the Mexican immigrants are targets of contradictory complaints, as with one voiced by a newspaper letter writer who referred to them as "lazy undesirables who clog the welfare rolls and take jobs held by Americans."

The facts give no comfort to this view. Indeed, they suggest just the opposite—that such immigration is a large plus for this country, a development we should be cheering, not deploring.

Migrants Are a Windfall

At least half a dozen studies on the impact of illegal Mexican immigration provide convincing evidence that these migrants pay heavy taxes (for which they receive no benefits), make scant use of welfare and other social services and contribute far more to the United States than they take from it. As social scientist Wayne Cornelius expressed it in a recent paper to a conference on Mexican immigration in San Diego:

"More generally, it could be argued that Mexican migrants represent something of a windfall for the United States, in the sense that they are young, highly productive workers, whose health care, education and other costs of rearing have been borne by Mexico, and whose maintenance during periods of unemployment and retirement (is) in Mexico. The significance of this windfall becomes more apparent when one considers that as of 1977 the cost of preparing a U.S.-born man or woman for integration into the U.S. labor force was about $44,000."

These migrants pay into the Social Security trust fund millions of dollars that they will never collect, as well as state income, sales and even property taxes for which they receive relatively few benefits. In the words of Douglas S. Massey of Princeton's Office of Population Research: "Far from ripping off the system, illegal aliens are more likely to be subsidizing it."

Culturally, Mexican migrants are reluctant to accept welfare, an attitude reinforced in the United States by fear of deportation if they apply for any social benefit.

In San Diego County, by far the largest entry point for Mexican migrants, a 1977-78 screening of welfare, Medi-Cal and food stamp recipients found only 317 illegal immigrants in a caseload of 285,000. A study by the Orange County Task Force in 1978, though weighted toward long-term illegals presumably more likely to use such services, found only 9 percent of them had received public medical care, only 2.8 percent had collected welfare payments and only 1.8 percent had received food stamps.

Illegals Pay Taxes

The Orange County Task Force estimated that illegal migrants in the county paid a minimum of $83 million in taxes annually while receiving medical services costing $2.7 million a year. A study by the Human Resources Agency of San Diego County discovered that the cost of all services for illegal migrants, including education, health care and welfare assistance, totaled $2 million a year. These same migrants contributed $48.8 million annually in taxes.

Illegal Immigrants Aid America

On balance, immigrants are far from a drag on the economy. As workers, consumers, entrepeneurs and taxpayers, they invigorate it and contribute healthy economic benefits. By increasing the work force, they also help solve our social security problem. Immigrants tend to come at the start of their work lives but when they retire and collect social security, they typically have raised children who are then contributing taxes to the system.

This country needs more, not fewer, immigrants. The U.S. birthrate is low and our future work force is shrinking. By opening our doors we will not only do good but the evidence indicates we will also do well.

Julian L. Simon, "Don't Close Our Borders," *Newsweek,* February 27, 1984.

These sorts of data prompt Mexican sociologist Jorge A. Bustamante to suggest that the proper term for describing illegals would be "undocumented taxpayers."

Another complaint against illegals is that they supposedly take jobs away from American workers or at least depress the labor market because, as U.S. Secretary of Labor Ray Marshall put it, they work "hard and scared." Undoubtedly there are instances, as in the current United Farm Workers strike in California's Salinas Valley, where illegal immigrants are placed in direct competition with American workers. But academic studies usually have concluded that fears of economic competition from illegals are greatly overstated.

This attitude is particularly evident in California, which is now enjoying the longest sustained economic boom in their history—a boom that coincides with heavy immigration, both legal and illegal. During this period, as Vilma Martinez, president of the

Mexican American Legal Defense and Education Fund, observes, the areas absorbing the greatest numbers of migrants also have had the lowest unemployment rates.

Illegals Are an Economic Benefit

The economic benefit to the United States of Mexican migration is best demonstrated by California agriculture, the most prosperous, diverse and specialized in the world. A few years ago, when Cesar Chavez was beginning to organize, his opponents complained that paying higher wage scales and granting the "industrial" benefits of unemployment insurance and health insurance to farm workers would make it impossible for California agriculture to compete.

Instead, these reforms have guaranteed California farmers a stable work force that is mostly Mexican or Mexican-American and that, because of the skills involved in such work as lettuce-harvesting, is largely irreplaceable by untrained Anglos.

While farm work is the largest single occupational category, more than half of the new immigrants head directly for the big cities, especially Los Angeles, where their entry into the labor market is apt to be at the bottom of the scale as dishwashers or busboys.

Because of the southern California business boom, there is a high demand even in these jobs. Furthermore, some 15 percent of the illegals may work in skilled or semiskilled construction jobs, according to one study, though they are more likely to be concentrated in unskilled heavy labor and domestic service and in janitorial, laundry, food processing, garment or shoe-factory jobs.

Illegals' Jobs Are Menial

Some economists believe that many of the service and domestic jobs performed by illegals simply wouldn't exist if the illegals weren't in the market. And some of the other jobs might not be there, either.

"Illegal aliens typically work in menial, low-paying positions shunned by citizens, who often work in supervisory and administrative positions in the same firms," Princeton's Massey writes. "If illegal aliens were unavailable, it is argued, these firms would either leave the country or go out of business, taking the supervisory and administrative positions held by American citizens with them."

Cornelius contends that the migrant is willing to take the "menial, unstable, dead-end position," because he is economically benefiting his family, "and because the absence of a long-term career ladder is not a disadvantage to the migrant who considers himself only a sojourner in the United States."

Typically, the Mexican migrant makes no distinction between "legal" and "illegal" immigration—and with good reason. Unlike

John Trevor, *The Alberquerque Journal.* Reprinted with permission.

immigrants from Europe and Asia, Mexicans lived in the area they are now emigrating to before the Anglo-Americans came. Geography and climate in Mexico and the U.S. Southwest are similar, access is relatively easy and the two countries are physically indistinguishable along much of the border.

The prevailing view among Mexicans seems to be that the illegals have every right to be in the United States, as indeed they did through much of U.S. history. The Border Patrol was not established until 1924, and entry without a visa did not become a crime until 1929.

Views of Mexican Border

From the beginning of the Western frontier, Anglo-Americans tended to regard Mexico as a vast labor reservoir that could be tapped and turned off at the asking. In prosperous, labor-short periods, such as during the two world wars, Mexican workers were recruited, subsidized and lavishly praised. But during three periods of slack labor markets (1920-21, 1930-35 and 1953-54), Mexican migrants were rounded up and deported, sometimes in actions so indiscriminate that legal U.S. citizens of Mexican origin were deported with them.

Bustamente maintains that the model of industry in the Southwest on both sides of the border reflects the reality of the large and growing Mexican labor pool. "On the U.S. side there is a real concrete need for cheap labor," he says. "On the Mexican side there is an increasing population, unfair distribution of income and a traditional pattern of migration to the United States. The border is not a place where realities end. It is a place where realities permeate. And we have to understand them in order to live together."

One pre-condition of that understanding is to recognize that migration from Mexico to the United States is here to stay, no matter what kind of fence is built on the border. Another would be to acknowledge that this immigration, in countless ways, is of real and lasting benefit to the United States.

"To recognize the undocumented immigrants and refugees as part of us is healthy and natural: they are here, rooted in our communities."

Amnesty Should Be Granted Illegal Aliens

The American Friends Service Committee

The American Friends Service Committee (AFSC) was founded in 1917 by the Religious Society of Friends (Quakers) but is supported and staffed by individuals of all denominations. The organization, a co-recipient of the Nobel Peace Prize, conducts work in seventeen countries to relieve human suffering and find new approaches to world peace and non-violent social change. In the following viewpoint, the AFSC gives their reasons for granting amnesty to illegal immigrants and concludes that since illegal immigration is impossible to control, amnesty is the only humane alternative.

As you read, consider the following questions:

1. How will amnesty eliminate exploitation of undocumented workers, according to AFSC?
2. Why does AFSC believe alternatives to amnesty unacceptable?
3. What are the five common objections to amnesty and how are they refuted by the AFSC?

Aurora Schmidt, "Legislation in the National Interest, 1983." Reprinted with permission of the American Friends Service Committee, 1501 Cherry Street, Philadelphia, PA, 19102.

From the earliest time of the immigration policy debate, legalization has been favored unanimously by every serious group and individual interested in better immigration laws....

Legalization will prevent exploitation and relieve suffering. The essential exploitability of undocumented workers is a threat to the whole social order. Its effects on wages, working conditions, labor organizing, housing and consumer prices permeate the broader society with highly negative impact. Acting INS Commissioner Doris Meissner testified to the House Subcommittee on Immigration that:

> Society is harmed every time an undocumented alien is afraid to testify as a witness in a legal proceeding—which occurs even if the alien is the victim—to report an illness that might constitute a public health hazard, or to disclose violations of U.S. labor laws.

Our experience is that most undocumented workers will not report labor law violations, from payment of less than minimum wages to the extremes of peonage.

Legalization is needed to ensure the rights of both immigrants and citizens. The existence of an exploitable class of people undermines the equality which we uphold as a value fundamental to our society and as the practical premise on which the rights of all rest. The abuses faced by the most exploitable can seldom be kept from spreading into the lives of the rest of us. The willingness of our people to allow a segment of the population to be deprived of civil and human rights and subjected to great hardship puts in great danger our abiding understanding that such abuses threaten the foundation of this country's rule of law and the carefully safeguarded principle of equality before it.

The alternatives are unacceptable. President Reagan's Omnibus Immigration Act of 1981 and the Immigration Reform and Control Act in both houses have based their recommendations for a legalization program on the impracticality and undesirability of massive repatriation. Many testimonies cited "Operation Wetback," which in 1954 deported over a million people to Mexico, as a shameful page in our history which must not be repeated. The report of the Select Commission on Immigration and Refugee Policy stated:

> Attempts at massive deportation would be destructive of U.S. liberties, costly, likely to be challenged in the courts and, in the end, ineffective. The only time in U.S. history when such a massive deportation effort occurred was in the mid-1950s when the Immigration and Naturalization Service (INS) expelled or repatriated more than 1 million aliens. This was done at tremendous cost in terms of both money and personnel, and, more importantly, it violated the civil liberties of many Mexican Americans who were forcibly repatriated to Mexico. Such an effort would not be tolerated today.

Regrettably, the U.S. government is now conducting a similar program, "Operation Jobs," a series of targeted raids in eight cities presented to the public as an experimental program to recapture jobs for legal residents and citizens. The results have not been jobs but abuses similar in scale and destructiveness to those of Operation Wetback. (The last section of this paper explores this new phenomenon more fully.) As pointed out by the Acting Commissioner of INS, "such an effort (massive repatriation) is unacceptable today. We believe that most people in the United States would not consider massive raids and deportation to be humane or in the national interest. Any immigration reform bill must ensure that it does not happen again."

Legalization is a practical measure. To remove people forcibly who are members of communities is difficult and painful. International relations can be seriously affected. It may cause hardship to U.S. citizens who are related to the undocumented person. It may take an inordinate amount of resources on the part of the Immigration and Naturalization Service. In addition, the restructuring and modernization of the INS would greatly benefit from a clean start....

For the AFSC, an inclusive legalization could have the function of bringing relief to a special class of people: unrecognized refugees. The

Reprinted with permission of the *Minneapolis Star and Tribune*.

problems of Central American immigrants and some Haitians who are here outside of a legal status will not be resolved by legalization alone. We agree with other religious groups which have called for the recognition, on the part of the United States, of the fact that Salvadorans, Guatemalans and Haitians are bona fide refugees under the United Nations definition. We continue to challenge the State Department's bias against this fact, based on foreign policy considerations. In the meantime we call for the most expeditious way of bringing relief to these refugees: to include them in the legalization plan. Senator Kennedy's amendment bringing the cut-off date to January 1982 was undoubtedly motivated in part by this realization.

At the present time the situation of Salvadorans, Guatemalans and Haitians outside of special status is untenable. The INS cannot possibly deal with the volume of political asylum petitions. The legal counsel representing these refugees have case loads bigger than is humanly possibly to handle. The refugee population has suffered prolonged detention, high bails, discrimination and all the evils of a clandestine existence. The present religious movement of sanctuary is proof of a widespread conviction in the communities of faith that laws dealing with these refugees are unjust and must be resisted. Legalization represents hope and constitutes a simple first step in the solution of the international embarrassment and the problem of conscience that the presence of some 400,000 unrecognized bona fide refugees in our midst is for the people of the United States....

Perceived Problems of Legalization

Several objections have been put forward with regard to a real legalization program:

1. The newly legalized will soon bring family members.

2. The impact on local communities is financially burdensome.

3. Legalization will create further job displacement of U.S. workers.

4. Legalization will congest the service-providing institutions, such as health and education systems.

5. Legalization is unfair to applicants for legal visas trapped in a backlog.

All of these objections are incorrect to a substantial degree.

1. The status of permanent residence only allows for the use of second preference in *family reunification*. The time span for naturalization is five years. In addition, a large segment of the undocumented population consists of immediate relatives who would not add to the secondary influx. However, it would be important to estimate family reunification effects of legalization, and to prepare for those numbers. In our opinion they will not add significantly to the volume of estimated respondents to legalization, which may well be a total of under two million. Most

spouses and children migrating to join newly legalized residents will not represent the need for new jobs.

2. The debate around the *impact of equalization on local communities* was resolved in the Senate through the allocation of block grants, and through a provision of 100% federal reimbursement to local governments in the House (Edwards amendment). We favor the latter, since the undocumented immigrants pay into the federal system. No cost estimates should discourage proponents of legalization. Undocumented workers have paid for it, by paying taxes and other contributions that until now cannot return in benefits to them as to other taxpayers.

Amnesty Is Compassionate

Several million undocumented aliens now reside in the United States. Both compassion and practicality require that those who have lived here long enough to acquire an "equity" in this nation be granted an amnesty leading to full citizenship. Compared to most immigration issues, amnesty is a popular cause.

William G. Hollingsworth, "On Immigration, First Things First," *Los Angeles Times,* March 23, 1984.

---

3. There is a general agreement that *legalization will not displace U.S. workers.* Quite the opposite: in the case of those employers who find their workforce suddenly legalized and therefore able to protect their labor rights, the incentive to hire undocumented workers will diminish (since all workers will be legal and the advantages of hiring the illegal worker over the legal competitor will be removed). A recent study done in California suggests that there is more competition between different segments of the undocumented workforce than between them and legal workers. This same study challenges the validity of the *Los Angeles Times* poll used to "prove" that legal workers are willing to do jobs presently held by undocumented workers.

4. In testimony to the House Subcommittee on Immigration, Doris Meissner, Acting Commissioner of the INS, reiterated that *the impact of the undocumented population on social services is to a large extent already being felt.* Referring to health services in particular, she added:

...the population we are talking about is largely a young population. It is overwhelmingly a working population and should not be very much of an additional burden on the health services structure in the U.S.

We believe that a small added strain on social services is well worth the benefits of legalization. In terms of health services, legalization is a net benefit to the community if we believe that, as in any group not receiving health care, there are likely to be undetected contagious diseases among immigrants who cannot seek help. Most testimonies given to the Select Commission by health service providers emphasized the desirability of protecting the health of the whole community and of the immigrants in particular. In the same vein, the recent court decision on the education of undocumented children in Texas stressed the overall benefits to society of including this class of people as early as possible in the system (education) that will most improve their chances of being productive and informed members of our society. During the trial, some witnesses presented estimates of possible added costs this inclusion would create. As in the case of economic impact on local governments, immigrants now pay indirectly for all these services.

5. *Legalization itself is not unfair for those trapped in the backlog* of applications for legal visas. We have suggested that any immigration reform must provide for an expeditious way to erase the backlog in family reunification quotas. Many people are victimized for the only reason that they came from the Dominican Republic or the Philippines. We have dealt with the matter of the justice of legalization. We cannot justify failure to do justice to one group because of unwillingness or inability to do justice to another group. The backlog is not in any way related to the size of the undocumented community....

The American Friends Service Committee wholeheartedly supports a real legalization program for undocumented immigrants. We think it is both desirable and possible. To recognize the undocumented immigrants and refugees as part of us is healthy and natural: they are here, rooted in our communities. To embrace their presence fully is to humbly accept that human events are larger than our capacity to understand them and control them. To extend a real legalization opportunity is to celebrate our common humanity with immigrants: a suffering people of great courage and strength.

"Amnesty is a bad precedent for our country to set. It shows our country is not serious about enforcing its immigration laws."

Amnesty Should Not Be Granted Illegal Aliens

F. James Sensenbrenner Jr.

F. James Sensenbrenner Jr., a United States Republican representative from Wisconsin, received a B.A. from Stanford University and a J.D. from the University of Wisconsin Law School. Since 1960 he has been actively involved in work for the Republican Party and was named Outstanding Young Republican in the Midwest in 1969. In a dissenting view given before the Congress on the proposed Immigration Reform and Control Act of 1983 that would grant amnesty to illegal aliens in the US. Mr. Sensenbrenner argues that amnesty is unfair to immigrants who attempt to legally enter the US.

As you read, consider the following questions:

1. What is "chain immigration" and why does Mr. Sensenbrenner believe it to be a major problem?
2. Why is amnesty too expensive, according to the author?
3. Why, according to the author, are employer sanctions needed?

F. James Sensenbrenner Jr., dissenting views in House Report 98-115, the proposed Immigration Reform and Control Act of 1983, issued on May 13, 1983.

House Report 1510 is nothing more than amnesty for millions upon millions of illegal aliens, permitting them to become permanent residents of the United States. There is no immigration reform—the system of legal immigration is scarcely mentioned in the bill. What little control there might have been in the bill has become so diluted that I fear it will only be a paperwork burden for employers, and a burdening of our Immigration and Naturalization Service that defies the imagination.

One of the major criticisms the American people have with the present immigration law is we have "different strokes for different folks" or different quotas for different people, resulting in no hard or fast limitation on how many foreigners are legally admitted into the United States on an annual basis. If a cap on legal immigration is not enacted, then the current number of legal immigrants entering our country will continue to mushroom. In 1982, legal immigration was over 435,000; add to that another 93,000 to 97,000 refugees admitted (depending on whose figures one uses) and you have legally added over one half million people to our population in one year's time.

Legal Immigration and US Economy

Legal immigration exploded at a time when our country could least afford it. Unemployment among U.S. citizens has been at an all time high. As our economy struggles to get back on its feet to provide for those who have been unemployed for months on end, it ill behooves us to purposely enact policies that will irritate and exacerbate this problem. The American people have soured on the entire issue of immigration, and the compassion Americans have felt toward refugees from oppression and political and religious persecution has become strained to the breaking point. Americans are having a difficult time understanding why our government continues to allow more people into this country who compete for jobs and place a drain on the treasuries of our state, local, and federal governments. Public opinion polls show that 80 percent of the American people want reductions in legal admissions. "Compassion fatigue" has, indeed, set in.

While some have argued that these are unsubstantiated fears, there are hard facts to support these concerns. For instance, a Presidential report in 1980 revealed that taxpayers have spent over $2 billion a year in refugee admissions. Billions of dollars more have been spent since this report was issued. These figures are put into greater perspective by a GAO report which showed that over 70 percent of the Indo-Chinese refugees of employable age had requested public assistance. Most requests were made within 30 days of arrival. In my own state of Wisconsin, which held more than 15,000 Cuban-Haitian refugees at Fort McCoy, I heard many complaints from both the state and local government officials strongly objecting to the open ended refugee policies.

117

Not only were these policies open ended, but state and local officials were unable to apprehend and return any refugee who escaped from Fort McCoy because they were not given authority to deal with these special people temporarily relocated in their area. These refugees ran the spectrum from honest, hardworking individuals who truly desired to escape to a free society, to hardened criminals released from jail and sent immediately to the United States. To add insult to injury, the full Committee rejected an amendment which would have urged the Attorney General to seek the active assistance of state and local law enforcement officials to provide immigration officers and the border patrol with desperately needed assistance.

Amnesty Encourages Illegal Immigration

Many amnestied aliens will bring relatives in once they have a secure immigration status and opportunities to obtain better jobs. Many illegal aliens are here simply to work and do not desire to become part of our society. Amnesty would make permanant settlement so attractive that many illegal aliens would decide to stay and send for parents, spouses, grandchildren, brothers and sisters, grandparents and the entire extended family of Third World cultures. And, in addition to the influx of relatives, as hundreds of thousands of amnestied aliens become American citizens in 1989 and subsequent years, they will begin to bring in immediate relatives subject to no numerical limitation.

Senator East, "From the Hopper," *The Review of the News,* January 19, 1984.

Placing refugees under the legal immigration cap is essential for our country to be able to withstand increasing pressure in the future for more refugee admissions. The current refugee explosion is only a preview of things to come. For instance, our world population will increase another two billion by the end of the century. This means the world labor force wil grow by 900,000,000 people, who will join some 50 million currently unemployed and 300 million underemployed. At the same time, economic and political tensions will add millions more. In other words, our country will be able to absorb only a small fraction of a percent of this number.

"Chain Immigration" Problem

A second problem affecting legal immigration concerns the method of allocating the admission of immigrants other than refugees into this country. H.R. 1510 does nothing to limit the 5th preference. The problem of "chain immigration," whereby alien brothers and sisters of U.S. citizens are given a preference for permanent residence, remains unchanged. Currently there is a 5th preference backlog of almost 900,000, and it is growing by leaps and bounds. Last year the backlog was 689,400 and in 1981, 551,800. Not only is the backlog growing, but the numbers processed have been decreasing. In 1982 alone, 207,705 5th preference applications were filed.

Since 1980, only 36 percent of the visas granted are for the actual brother or sister of the applicant. All the rest are for the spouses and children of the beneficiary. In simple English, 3 of 8 applicants are the principal beneficiaries of 5th preference, and 5 of 8 are not. If the 5th preference is not modified, then closer family members, i.e., spouses, sons, and daughters, will continue to have problems being united. If family reunification is to be preferred public policy, it should be for the closest relatives—not a loophole to bring "every" relative into the country.

Because of the way in which the preference system is allocated, family reunification is becoming the principal way for immigrants, other than refugees, to enter this country. This will be felt even more a few years down the road when all the legal immigrants, which includes refugees, become citizens; and, if amnesty is granted, the millions of now illegal aliens will be eligible for citizenship, and naturally will want to bring their relatives into this country. As the "spill down" from other preference categories declines, fewer and fewer 5th preference visas will be processed. It is not unreasonable to project that in a few short years, the only 5th preference visas processed will be the numbers allocated—64,000 (24 percent of 270,000). Then what kind of a backlog will there be? What incentive will there be to wait in line for legal immigration?

The most objectionable feature of H.R. 1510, however, is the provision which grants amnesty to unknown millions of illegal aliens.

Hidden Costs of Amnesty

The costs of the amnesty bill are unclear because it is not known how many illegal aliens will take advantage of this program. Last year the CBO estimated the number of illegal aliens to be 4.5 million; the Justice Department estimates the number to be 5 million; and other estimates vary from 8 to 10 to 12 million illegal aliens. Obviously, the costs will be astronomical. All these costs will be absorbed by either the federal, state, or local governments, some of which are already subject to enormous pressure to cut their budgets and reduce their spending. These additional costs could bankrupt some of these jurisdictions in the next few years. If as some people claim, only about one-half the eligible illegal aliens come forward and apply for legalization, that still leaves a sizable population of illegal aliens, and renders the entire program as an expensive exercise in futility.

Aside from the billions of dollars of increased costs to the federal, state, and local governments, there are numerous other reasons for opposing this legislative program.

The legalization program has no safeguards. It does not provide protection against aliens purchasing false documents, i.e., leases, affidavits, etc., to prove they have been in this country the required number of years. In addition, the amnesty program will be an incentive for more illegal aliens to enter our country. The limitations as to who will be eligible for amnesty will not filter down to the citizens residing in economically depressed countries. They will only hear that amnesty is being granted and the influx will start.

Amnesty Increases Population

Amnesty would establish a dangerous precedent that can only encourage more illegal immigration. Future waves of illegal aliens will join their "legalized" friends and relatives. They will expect to receive the same treatment as the first wave, and the aliens will clamor for those friends and relatives.

The reasons given today to justify amnesty—impracticability and inhumanity of mass deportations—will be used again and again to justify future programs.

Palmer Stacy, "'Amnesty' Is No Solution for Illegal Aliens," *Human Events*, June 19, 1982.

Amnesty is a bad precedent for our country to set. It shows our country is not serious about enforcing its immigration laws. It truly makes our borders in the southwest borderless. Aliens will continue to come to the United States hoping in the future they, too, will be granted amnesty.

Incentives for Illegals

I fear that the U.S. Supreme Court decision rendered in *Plyler, Superintendent, Tyler Independent School District et al.* v. *Doe, Guardian,* which forced the state of Texas to provide free education benefits to children of illegal aliens, will be extended to include other benefits. This is yet another incentive for a family to move illegally to the United States.

The employer sanctions in the bill are equally ineffective. Illegal aliens drawn by the "economic magnet" to the U.S. will not be hindered. Supporters of the bill will argue the employer sanctions will turn off the "economic magnet." However, this is not true. The employer sanctions were considerably weakened in the full Judiciary Committee. The burden of proof in enforcement of immigration laws has now been shifted from the government to the employer. Employer sanctions must be stronger for the magnet to be turned off. Illegal aliens must not have an incentive to come or to stay in this country.

Blanket amnesty is unfair to the over one million immigrant applicants, some of whom have been waiting as long as 12 years to come to this country legally, and still don't know how much longer they will have to wait. We are saying to these people, they were stupid for obeying the law. If they had come here illegally, they would be rewarded. However, because they decided to abide by our law, they are penalized. We are keeping law abiding applicants out of the country while giving resident status to lawbreakers.

I would hope the U.S. could continue as much as possible its "open door" tradition and policy toward the displaced, the persecuted, and the ambitious of the world. However, the reality of our economic and resource situation is that we simply cannot continue to be a nation without borders. We must limit the influx of aliens and immigrants and have an orderly and fair system for admitting those we are able to absorb.

"To deny children the opportunity to develop their own language is to condemn them to playing catch-up for the rest of their educational lives."

Bilingual Education Is Beneficial

Raúl Yzaguirre

Raúl Yzaguirre is a civil rights administrator. He earned a B.S. from George Washington University. Active in the War on Poverty from 1969-74, Mr. Yzaguirre is currently president of the National Council of La Raza as well as chairperson of The Neighborhood Coalition and co-chairman of the National Committee on Concerns of Hispanics and Blacks. In the following viewpoint Mr. Yzaguirre proposes that the only way of integrating non-English speakers into society and ending the high drop-out rate among Hispanics is through bilingual education.

As you read, consider the following questions:

1. Why, according to Mr. Yzaguirre, is bilingual education a major civil rights issue?
2. What is the goal of bilingual education, according to the author?
3. Why are arguments that bilingual education leads to separatism false, according to the author?

Raul Yzaguirre, "Bilingual Education: The Key to Equal Opportunity," *Agenda*, March/April 1981. Reprinted with permission of the National Council of La Raza, 20 F St. NW, 2nd Fl., Washington, DC 20001.

In the 25 years that I have spent in the Civil Rights Movement, I have seen many legitimate issues misrepresented, misconstrued, deliberately framed in such a way as to undermine their true goals, and otherwise cast in terms that arouse passionate opposition. But never in that time have I seen the press and the politicians so united in the use of these tactics as they have been on the issue of bilingual education.

Bilingual education is one of the major civil rights issues of the 1980s, a fact which seems to be missed by the media and those officials involved in deciding whether the concept of bilingual education lives or dies in this country. Yet there is no doubt that the educational problems faced by non-English-speaking children in this country, *the vast majority of whom are not newly arrived immigrants,* are the direct result of segregation and discriminatory treatment dating back over a century.

The issue of providing bilingual education to all language minority children is, by its very nature, a complicated issue and thus lends itself to misrepresentation and misinterpretation. There are aspects of the issue on which reasonable people may, with all good intentions, disagree. But the essential elements are quite clear and the need, indeed the legal mandate, for meeting the educational requirements of the 3.5 million children in this country whose primary language is other than English is unquestionable, although frequently omitted from the debates.

Facts Support Bilingualism

Let us begin with the basic facts. The use of traditional instruction methods to teach cognitive subjects in English to non-English-speaking children has never worked, is not working now, and will never work. The need for a different approach has been overwhelmingly supported by statistical evidence which shows that:

- out of every 100 children who enter school, 14 Anglos and 33 Blacks will not complete high school, but *40* Chicanos and Puerto Ricans will not;
- one-third of Chicanos and Puerto Ricans 25 years and older have not completed high school;
- about one of four Chicanos and Puerto Ricans have less than five years of formal education;
- Chicanos and Puerto Ricans have a 100 percent greater chance of being expelled from school than Anglos;
- the number of Chicanos who are held back at least one year is eight times greater than Anglos.

The old arguments used to account for this lopsided failure of the school systems to provide adequate education to Hispanics no longer hold water: "Educational disparity among Hispanics is due to genetic differences"; "They're clannish and like to stay in their own *barrios* and speak their own language" (as in, "Jews and Blacks *like* to live in their ghettoes"); "If the waves of alien hordes would stop coming there would be no language problem." Any intelligent person has discarded these assumptions like worn-out shoes, but there are many who continue to blame the victim rather than deal with the causes.

Bilingual Education Gets Results

Bilingual education effectively meets the needs of linguistic-minority children. It respects what the children themselves bring to the classroom—their language and culture....Participants in bilingual-education programs are four times as likely to finish school, and the number entering college has increased.

Another gain from preserving native languages is that the United States now has more linguistic resources for its diplomatic dealings with other countries—Vietnam, El Salvador and the Middle East, for example.

Ramón Santiago, "Teach Immigrants in Their Own Language," *U.S. News & World Report,* October 3, 1983.

Although many languages are represented among linguistically different children, over 70 percent of the children at risk are Hispanic. Studies spanning nearly half a century have consistently shown that Hispanics are the nation's most undereducated minority, and the statistics quoted above attest to that fact. To put it another way, monolingual, English-only instruction has had at least as devastating an effect educationally on Hispanics as slavery and segregation had on Blacks. The recent decision by Chief Judge Wayne Justice in *U.S. vs. Texas* pointed to the states long history of unconstitutional discrimination against Hispanics as an unlawful impediment to equal educational opportunity for Hispanic students. The ruling caps ten years of litigation and is especially remarkable since the State of Texas conceded that its past practices, especially as regards language policy, contributed significantly to present problems.

The Meaning of Bilingual

Opponents of bilingual education seem to have difficulty understanding the English language themselves. Bilingual means *two* languages. Proponents want bilingual education *precisely* because they believe, and the evidence supports, that this approach is the best method of assuring competency, both linguistic and conceptual, in English. Pedagogically speaking, the concept of bilingual education is rooted in basic common sense, for basic to all precepts of teaching is that one builds on the foundation of what the child brings to the classroom. And for 3.5

million children in this country, what they bring to the classroom is a language other than English.

To deny children the opportunity to develop their own language is to condemn them to playing catch-up for the rest of their educational lives. In essence, what the public education system has been saying to linguistically different children is: "What you know is worthless; what you are is worthless; you do not fit our norm, and we have no responsibility to accommodate your needs."

Unfortunately, it is not the pedagogical or civil rights aspects of bilingual education that are discussed in the media or the political debates. What is suggested, often in the most xenophobic of terms, is that "foreigners" refuse to become "American," that somehow bilingualism will lead to political and social separatism, or that the federal government is intruding on local and states rights.

Indians Are Not Foreigners

How the descendents of the first Americans (Native Indians), or the first Europeans to settle in this hemisphere and on this continent (Hispanics) can now be classified as foreigners is a little confusing. This is especially so since, at least in the cases of the Southwestern part of the United States and Puerto Rico, pre-existing Spanish-speaking populations were absorbed into the United States not through free immigration, but rather through war or other political experiences. The language and culture of Hispanics are as deeply imbedded in U.S. history as are Puritanism and the English language.

Advocates of bilingual education have a clear goal: full literacy in both an individual's home language and in English. The message is one of connecting, bridging, unifying the two cultural worlds through language, not separation or isolation from the mainstream. Some opponents point to events in Canada and the desire of some French-speaking Canadians to become a separate political entity as a dark spectre of the future and an argument against bilingual education. The lessons of Canada are instructive, but not in the ways suggested by the media and the political demagogues. French separatists are not interested in bilingual education. They want monolingual instruction only in French. The true enemies of Canadian political and social unity are the linguistic and cultural chauvinists, some of whom are French and others of whom are Anglo....

A Paranoid Nation

Have we become as a nation so paranoid that we are frightened by the prospect of a few of our children developing their full potential? Is our unity as a people so fragile that we must homogenize every child into some contrived notion of what an

American should be and then label that child a failure when he or she does not measure up to that standard? Have we developed such a siege mentality that we cannot grasp the rich rewards of having Americans who can better relate to the rest of the world because of the experience of learning in more than one language and culture?

I fervently hope not.

"The bilingualists simplistically scorn the value and necessity of assimilation."

Bilingual Education Is Harmful

Richard Rodriguez

Richard Rodriguez, the son of working-class Mexican immigrants, was raised in Sacramento, California. Educated at Stanford and Columbia Universities, he did graduate work at the Warburg Institute in London and the University of California in Berkeley. Mr. Rodriguez is a writer and lecturer, and his essays have appeared in *The American Scholar, College English,* and *Change* magazine. In *Hunger of Memory,* his autobiography and the source for this viewpoint, Mr. Rodriguez deals with the controversial policies of affirmative action and bilingualism in education. Here, he speaks against bilingual education, believing that it delays assimilation and harms non-English speaking children's self-identity by allowing them to remain a separate group from their English speaking peers.

As you read, consider the following questions:

1. Why does the author believe his own childhood isolation is not an argument for bilingual education?
2. Why does the author believe that black English is not an appropriate language to be taught in?
3. According to the author, why do supporters of public bilingualism "sin against intimacy"?

An accident of geography sent me to a school where all my classmates were white, many the children of doctors and lawyers and business executives. All my classmates certainly must have been uneasy on that first day of school—as most children are uneasy—to find themselves apart from their families in the first institution of their lives. But I was astonished.

The nun said, in a friendly but oddly impersonal voice, 'Boys and girls, this is Richard Rodriguez.' (I heard her sound out: *Rich-heard Road-ree-guess.*) It was the first time I had heard anyone name me in English. 'Richard,' the nun repeated more slowly, writing my name down in her black leather book. Quickly I turned to see my mother's face dissolve in a watery blur behind the pebbled glass door.

Many years later there is something called bilingual education—a scheme proposed in the late 1960s by Hispanic-American social activists, later endorsed by a congressional vote. It is a program that seeks to permit non-English-speaking children, many from lower-class homes, to use their family language as the language of school. (Such is the goal its supporters announce.) I hear them and am forced to say no: It is not possible for a child—any child—ever to use his family's language in school. Not to understand this is to misunderstand the public uses of schooling and to trivialize the nature of intimate life—a family's 'language.'...

Supporters of bilingual education today imply that students like me miss a great deal by not being taught in their family's language. What they seem not to recognize is that, as a socially disadvantaged child, I considered Spanish to be a private language. What I needed to learn in school was that I had the right—and the obligation—to speak the public language of *los gringos*. The odd truth is that my first-grade classmates could have become bilingual, in the conventional sense of that word, more easily than I. Had they been taught (as upper-middle-class children are often taught early) a second language like Spanish or French, they could have regarded it simply as that: another public language. In my case such bilingualism could not have been so quickly achieved. What I did not believe was that I could speak a single public language.

Delaying English

Without question, it would have pleased me to hear my teachers address me in Spanish when I entered the classroom. I would have felt much less afraid. I would have trusted them and responded with ease. But I would have delayed—for how long postponed?—having to learn the language of public society. I would have evaded—and for how long could I have afforded to delay?—learning the great lesson of school, that I had a public identity.

Fortunately, my teachers were unsentimental about their responsibility. What they understood was that I needed to speak a public language. So their voices would search me out, asking me questions. Each time I'd hear them, I'd look up in surprise to see a nun's face frowning at me. I'd mumble, not really meaning to answer. The nun would persist, 'Richard, stand up. Don't look at the floor. Speak up. Speak to the entire class, not just to me!' But I couldn't believe that the English language was mine to use. (In part, I did not want to believe it.) I continued to mumble. I resisted the teacher's demands. (Did I somehow suspect that once I learned a public language my pleasing family life would be changed?) Silent, waiting for the bell to sound, I remained dazed, diffident, afraid.

Learning English Is Vital

The experience of many immigrants shows that the more quickly they are immersed in the use of the English language, whether at work or at school, the more quickly they learn English—and I believe it is vital that they do so. This is generally true for immigrants of practically any age, and it's especially true of small children....

No immigrant group, no matter how large, has ever made a claim for special treatment such as bilingual education. Even among the Spanish speaking, the rank and file do not seem to be making that demand.

S.I. Hayakawa, "Teach Immigrants in Their Own Language?" *U.S. News & World Report*, October 3, 1983.

Because I wrongly imagined that English was intrinsically a public language and Spanish an intrinsically private one, I easily noted the difference between classroom language and the language of home. At school, words were directed to a general audience of listeners. ('Boys and girls.') Words were meaningfully ordered. And the point was not self-expression alone but to make oneself understood by many others. The teacher quizzed: 'Boys and girls, why do we use that word in this sentence? Could we think of a better word to use there? Would the sentence change its meaning if the words were differently arranged? And wasn't there a better way of saying much the same thing?' (I couldn't say. I wouldn't try to say.)

Three months. Five. Half a year passed. Unsmiling, ever watchful, my teachers noted my silence. They began to connect my behavior with the difficult progress my older sister and brother were making. Until one Saturday morning three nuns arrived at the house to talk to our parents. Stiffly, they sat on the blue living room sofa. From the doorway of another room, spying the visitors, I noted the incongruity—the clash of two worlds, the faces and voices of school intruding upon the familiar setting of home. I overheard one voice gently wondering, 'Do your children speak only Spanish at home, Mrs. Rodriguez?' While another voice added, 'that Richard especially seems so timid and shy.

That Rich-heard!

"En Ingles"

With great tact the visitors continued, 'Is it possible for you and your husband to encourage your children to practice their English when they are home?' Of course, my parents complied. What would they not do for their children's well-being? And how could they have questioned the Church's authority which those women represented? In an instant, they agreed to give up the language (the sounds) that had revealed and accentuated our family's closeness. The moment after the visitors left, the change was observed. *'Ahora,* speak to us *en ingles,'* my father and mother united to tell us.

At first, it seemed a kind of game. After dinner each night, the family gathered to practice 'our' English. (It was still then *ingles,* a language foreign to us, so we felt drawn as strangers to it.) Laughing, we would try to define words we could not pronounce. We played with strange English sounds, often overanglicizing our pronunciations. And we filled the smiling gaps of our sentences with familiar Spanish sounds. But that was cheating, somebody shouted. Everyone laughed. In school, meanwhile, like my brother and sister, I was required to attend a daily tutoring session. I needed a full year of special attention. I also needed my teachers to keep my attention from straying in class by calling out, *Rich-heard*—their English voices slowly prying loose my ties to my other name, its three notes, *Ri-car-do.* Most of all I needed to hear my mother and father speak to me in a moment of seriousness in broken—suddenly heartbreaking—English. The scene was inevitable: One Saturday morning I entered the kitchen where my parents were talking in Spanish. I did not realize that they were talking in Spanish. I did not realize that they were talking in Spanish however until, at the moment they saw me, I heard their voices change to speak English. Those *gringo* sounds they uttered startled me. Pushed me away. In that moment of trivial misunderstanding and profound insight, I felt my throat twisted by unsounded grief. I turned quickly and left the room. But I had no place to escape to with Spanish. (The spell was broken.) My brother and sisters were speaking English in another part of the house.

Again and again in the days following, increasingly angry, I was obliged to hear my mother and father: 'Speak to us *en ingles.'* *(Speak.)* Only then did I determine to learn classsroom English. Weeks after, it happened: One day in school I raised my hand to volunteer an answer. I spoke out in a loud voice. And I did not think it remarkable when the entire class understood. That day, I moved very far from the disadvantaged child I had been only days earlier. The belief, the calming assurance that I belonged in public, had at last taken hold.

Shortly after, I stopped hearing the high and loud sounds of *los gringos*. A more and more confident speaker of English, I didn't trouble to listen to *how* strangers sounded, speaking to me. And there simply were too many English-speaking people in my day for me to hear American accents anymore. Conversations quickened. Listening to persons who sounded eccentrically pitched voices, I usually noted their sounds for an initial few seconds before I concentrated on *what* they were saying. Conversations became content-full. Transparent. Hearing someone's *tone* of voice—angry or questioning or sarcastic or happy or sad—I didn't distinguish it from the words it expressed. Sound and word were thus tightly wedded. At the end of a day, I was often bemused, always relieved, to realize how 'silent,' though crowded with words, my day in public had been. (This public silence measured and quickened the change in my life.)

At last, seven years old, I came to believe what had been technically true since my birth; I was an American citizen....

The Necessity of Assimilation

Today I hear bilingual educators say that children lose a degree of 'individuality' by becoming assimilated into public society. (Bilingual schooling was popularized in the seventies, that decade when middle-class ethnics began to resist the process of assimilation—the American melting pot.) But the bilingualists simplistically scorn the value and necessity of assimilation. They do not seem to realize that there are *two* ways a person is individualized. So they do not realize that while one suffers a diminished sense of *private* individuality by becoming assimilated into public society, such assimilation makes possible the achievement of *public* individuality.

The bilingualists insist that a student should be reminded of his difference from others in mass society, his heritage. But they equate mere separateness with individuality. The fact is that only in private—with intimates—is separateness from the crowd a prerequisite for individuality. (An intimate draws me apart, tells me that I am unique, unlike all others.) In public, by contrast, full individuality is achieved, paradoxically, by those who are able to consider themselves members of the crowd. Thus it happened for me: Only when I was able to think of myself as an American, no longer an alien in *gringo* society, could I seek the rights and opportunities necessary for full public individuality. The social and political advantages I enjoy as a man result from the day that I came to believe that my name, indeed, is *Rich-heard Road-ree-guess.* It is true that my public society today is often impersonal. (My public society is usually mass society.) Yet despite the anonymity of the crowd and despite the fact that the individuality I achieve in public is often tenuous—because it depends on my being one in a crowd—I celebrate the day I acquired my new name. Those middle-class ethnics who scorn assimilation seem to me filled with decadent self-pity, obsessed by the burden of public life. Dangerously, they romanticize public separateness and they trivialize the dilemma of the socially disadvantaged.

Inevitable Pain

My awkward childhood does not prove the necessity of bilingual education. My story discloses instead an essential myth of childhood—inevitable pain. If I rehearse here the changes in my private life after my Americanization, it is finally to emphasize the public gain. The loss implies the gain: The house I returned to each afternoon was quiet. Intimate sounds no longer rushed to the door to greet me. There were other noises inside. The telephone rang. Neighborhood kids ran past the door of the bedroom where I was reading my schoolbooks—covered with shopping-bag paper. Once I learned public language, it would never again be easy for me to hear intimate family voices. More and more of my day was spent hearing words. But that may only be a way of saying that the day I raised my hand in class and spoke loudly to an entire roomful of faces, my childhood started to end....

No Evidence Supporting Bilingual Education

Proponents of bilingual education argue that classes taught in a child's native tongue enable that child to acquire fundamental skills while learning English. English in fact is easier to learn by a Spanish route, it is said. Becoming literate in a simpler language—one which is written as it sounds—eases the task of mastering one that is more complex. But there is no evidence that children in bilingual classes progress faster than peers with comparable language difficulties who are placed in regular classrooms or receive remedial help in English. The most important evidence that we have suggests otherwise.

Abigail M. Thernstrom, "Bilingual Mis-Education," *The New Republic,* April 18, 1981.

Intimacy continued at home; intimacy was not stilled by English. It is true that I would never forget the great change of my life, the diminished occasions of intimacy. But there would also be times when I sensed the deepest truth about language and intimacy: *Intimacy is not created by a particular language; it is created by*

132

intimates. The great change in my life was not linguistic but social. If, after becoming a successful student, I no longer heard intimate voices as often as I had earlier, it was because I spoke English rather than Spanish. It was because I used public language for most of the day. I moved easily at last, a citizen in a crowded city of words....

I remember the black political activists who have argued in favor of using black English in schools. (Their argument varies only slightly from that day by foreign-language bilingualists.) I have heard 'radical' linguists make the point that black English is a complex and intricate version of English. And I do not doubt it. But neither do I think that black English should be a language of public instruction. What makes black English inappropriate in classrooms is not something *in* the language. It is rather what lower-class speakers make of it. Just as Spanish would have been a dangerous language for me to have used at the start of my education, so black English would be a dangerous language to use in the schooling of teenagers for whom it reenforces feelings of public separateness.

Retaining Individuality

This seems to me an obvious point. But one that needs to be made. In recent years there have been attempts to make the language of the alien public language. 'Bilingual education, two ways to understand...,' television and radio commercials glibly announce. Proponents of bilingual education are careful to say that they want students to acquire good schooling. Their argument goes something like this: Children permitted to use their family language in school will not be so alienated and will be better able to match the progress of English-speaking children in the crucial first months of instruction. (Increasingly confident of their abilities, such children will be more inclined to apply themselves to their studies in the future.) But then the bilingualists claim another, very different goal. They say that children who use their family language in school will retain a sense of their individuality—their ethnic heritage and cultural ties. Supporters of bilingual education thus want it both ways. They propose bilingual schooling as a way of helping students acquire the skills of the classroom crucial for public success. But they likewise insist that bilingual instruction will give students a sense of their identity apart from the public.

Behind this screen there gleams an astonishing promise: One can become a public person while still remaining a private person. At the very same time one can be both! There need be no tension between the self in the crowd and the self apart from the crowd! Who would not want to believe such an idea? Who can be surprised that the scheme has won the support of many middle-class Americans? If the barrio or ghetto child can retain his separateness even while being publicly educated, then it is almost possible to believe that there is no private cost to be paid for public success. Such is the consolation offered by any of the current bilingual schemes. Consider, for example, the bilingual voters' ballot. In some American cities one can cast a ballot printed in several languages. Such a document implies that a person can exercise that most public of rights—the right to vote—while still keeping apart, unassimilated from public life.

Words as Family Ties

It is not enough to say that these schemes are foolish and certainly doomed. Middle-class supporters of public bilingualism toy with the confusion of those Americans who cannot speak standard English as well as they can. Bilingual enthusiasts, moreover, sin against intimacy. An Hispanic-American writer tells me, 'I will never give up my family language; I would as soon give up my soul.' Thus he holds to his chest a skein of words, as though it were the source of his family ties. He credits to language what he should credit to family members. A convenient mistake. For as long as he holds on to words, he can ignore how much else has changed in his life.

Recognizing Stereotypes

A stereotype is an oversimplified or exaggerated description of people or things. Stereotyping can be favorable. However, most stereotyping tends to be highly uncomplimentary and, at times, degrading.

Stereotyping grows out of our prejudices. When we stereotype someone, we are prejudging him or her. Consider the following example: Mr. X is convinced that all immigrants receive a "free ride" from the government. The Kaos, a family of Hmongs, happen to be his next-door neighbors. One Sunday afternoon, Mr. X notices that Mr. Kao has driven into his driveway in a brand new LeBaron. While Mr. Kao's family admires the new car Mr. X says to himself: "If it weren't for all that money they get from welfare they'd never be able to afford that new car." The possibility that Mr. Kao's entire family pitched in to buy the car, or even that Mr. Kao took out a huge bank loan to afford the car never enters into his mind. Why not? Simply because he has prejudged all immigrants and will keep his stereotype consistent with his prejudice.

The following statements relate to the subject matter in this chapter. Consider each statement carefully. *Mark S for any statement that is an example of stereotyping. Mark U if you are undecided about any statement.*

If you are doing this activity as a member of a class or group, compare your answers with those of other class or group members. Be able to defend your answers. You may discover that others will come to different conclusions than you. Listening to the reasons others present for their answers may give you valuable insights in recognizing stereotypes.

If you are reading this book alone, ask others if they agree with your answers. You too will find this interaction very valuable.

S = *stereotype*
N = *not a stereotype*
U = *undecided*

135

1. Mexican-Americans have large families.

2. Many Mexican migrants pay heavy taxes and make scant use of welfare and other social services.

3. Illegal immigrants are a drain on the American workers.

4. Illegal immigrants take needed jobs from American workers.

5. Cuban and Haitian refugees are responsible for the high crime rate in Miami, Florida.

6. Immigrants increase the US population growth by 50%.

7. People who favor uncontrolled immigration are humanitarians.

8. Illegal immigrants are exploited by their employers.

9. America is a land of immigrants.

10. Refugees are responsible for higher taxes.

11. Most immigrants are more hardworking than their citizen counterparts.

12. Immigrants are flagrant welfare abusers.

13. Current immmigration laws only benefit the wealthy and talented immigrants.

14. Educational disparity among Hispanics is due to genetic differences.

15. Many Hispanic-American children have difficulty learning English.

16. Bilingual education is only one way that foreigners avoid becoming Americans.

17. Immigrants add ethnic diversity to American culture.

18. Immigrants who don't learn English are not true Americans.

19. Blacks are at a disadvantage in the job market if they only speak black English.

Periodical Bibliography

The following list of periodical articles deals with the subject matter of this chapter.

Jim Bates — "US Immigration Policy," *The Humanist*, November/December 1981.

Tom Bethel — "Illegal Agreements," *National Review*, June 25, 1982.

William Chaze — "Invasion From Mexico," *U.S. News & World Report*, March 7, 1983.

Congressional Digest — "Should Congress Adopt the Pending 'Immigration Reform and Control Act'?" August/September 1983.

Georges Fauriol — "US Immigration Policy and The National Interest," *The Humanist*, May/June 1984.

Geoffrey Fox — "Inferior Status," *The Nation*, September 1981.

Ed Griffin — "Help Mexican Workers at Home," *The Nation*, March 3, 1984.

Sylvia Ann Hewlett — "Coping With Illegal Immigrants," *Foreign Affairs*, Winter 1981-82.

Karen Klein — "Citizens in All but Name," *Newsweek*, May 31, 1982.

Carl Migdal — "Mexico's Poverty: Driving Force for Border Jumpers," *U.S. News & World Report*, March 7, 1983.

Jonathon Rowe — "Murder By Deportation," *The Washington Monthly*, February 1984.

Ramon Santiago — "Teach Immigrants in Their Own Language," *U.S. News & World Report*, October 3, 1983.

Julian L. Simon — "In Favor of Immigration," *Inquiry*, April 1983.

Abigail Therbstrom — "Bilingual Mis-education," *New Republic*, April 18, 1981.

U.S. News & World Report — "It's the Immigrants Who Can Move Dramatically," July 4, 1983.

U.S. News & World Report — "Punish Employers of Illegal Aliens," March 23, 1981.

Do Women Receive
Equal Treatment?

"An economic program that speaks to the needs of women will have to address some of the most deep-seated injustices of a business-dominated economy and a male-dominated society."

Women Are Economically Exploited

Barbara Ehrenreich and Karin Stallard

Barbara Ehrenreich is a journalist and contributing editor to *Ms.* magazine. She is the author of *The Hearts of Men* and co-author of *For Her Own Good.* Karin Stallard is a writer in Brooklyn, New York. A grant from the Windom Fund along with research assistance from the Institute for Policy Studies in Washington, D.C. was provided Ms. Ehrenreich and Ms. Stallard for the preparation of a major article they co-authored for *Ms.* In the following viewpoint, excerpted from that article, the authors explain why they believe that the male-dominated corporate and societal power structure is contributing to the "feminization of poverty."

As you read, consider the following questions:

1. According to sociologist Diana Pearce, what is meant by the "feminization of poverty"?
2. What is meant by the "enterprise zone"?
3. According to the authors, what is the difficulty a feminist economic program will face?

Barbara Ehrenreich and Karin Stallard, "The Nouveau Poor," *Ms.*, July/August 1982. Reprinted with permission of the author.

Avis Strong Parke lives in a summer house on Cape Cod, but when we visited her it was not summer and the wind cutting across the bay shook the plastic covering on the windows and turned her breath white as she spoke. "We don't have any heat," she apologized, almost compensating for the cold with her smile. "You get used to that. The real problem is that the pipes tend to freeze and crack." Her outfit gave us a new perspective on the price of plumbing repairs: trousers outgrown by one teenage son, shoes worn out by another, and thermal underwear shared with another of her six children, three of whom still live at home with her. In her own phrase, Avis is one of the "nouveau poor": middle class by birth and marriage, she is now raising her three youngest children on a tenuous combination of welfare, child support, and her native Yankee ingenuity.

Most people know that the poor, with what the Administration calls their "runaway entitlements," are slated to take the brunt of the federal budget cuts. What most people do not know is that today, more than at any time in recent history, the poor are likely to be women. Two out of three adults who fall into the federal definition of poverty are women, and more than half the families defined as poor are maintained by single women. In the mid-sixties and until the mid-seventies, the number of poor adult males declined, while the number of poor women heading households swelled by 100,000 a year, prompting the National Advisory Council on Economic Opportunity to predict:

All other things being equal, if the proportion of the poor in female-householder families were to continue to increase at the same rate as it did from 1967 to 1978, the poverty population would be composed solely of women and their children before the year 2000.

The Feminization of Poverty

The grim economic news belies the image of the seventies as women's "decade of liberation." For some women, in some ways, it was. Women who were young, educated, and enterprising beat a path into once-closed careers like medicine, law, college teaching, and middle management. In the media, the old feminine ideal of the suburban housewife with 2.3 children and a station wagon was replaced by the upwardly mobile career woman with attache case and skirted suit. Television "anchorwomen" became as familiar as yesterday's news, chairmen became chairpersons, so that at times it seemed as if the only thing holding back *any* woman was a subnormal supply of "assertiveness." But, underneath the upbeat images, women as a class—young, old, black, white—were steadily losing ground, with those who were doubly disadvantaged, black and Hispanic women, taking the heaviest losses.

Sociologist Dr. Diana Pearce, who first flagged the trend in a

1978 article, calls it "the feminization of poverty," and if the phrase is not yet a household expression, it may be because public officials are loath to advertise the fact that the prime victims of service cutbacks are women—women and their dependent children. According to Pearce, the trend is accelerating. Between 1978 and 1980, the number of women who head households recruited into poverty rose to 150,000 per year, and there is every reason to think it will continue to increase. The feminization of poverty—or, to put it the other way, the impoverishment of women—may be the most crucial challenge facing feminism today....

The Feminization of Poverty

Despite the widespread misperception that women are achieving economic equality, their economic status has deteriorated sharply since the late 1960s. Today women—and children—are the primary beneficiaries of social welfare programs for the poor....By 1980, America's poor were predominantly female; two out of three adults whose incomes fell below the official federal poverty line were women, and more than half the families who were poor were headed by women.

Barbara Ehrenreich and Frances Fox Piven, *Dissent*, Spring 1984.

The New Right's solution to the feminization of poverty is, as you may have deduced, marriage. (Actually, none of the New Right spokespeople we interviewed was aware of the statistics on women and poverty, so the "solutions" were only elicited after a short briefing.) Onalee McGraw, who handles education and family issues at the influential Heritage Foundation (the New Right think tank, initially bankrolled by beer magnate Joseph Coors in 1973), rejects economic solutions such as efforts to increase women's earnings. "The priorities would be out of whack," she explained, since her first priority is to make men productive workers and reliable husbands. "I don't oppose equal pay for women," she told us, "but it could possibly exacerbate the whole situation in the long run . . . Anything that's more likely to make a woman more independent, more of a powerhouse, more of a threat to men, is not going to help." Her solution? "We need to make it tougher for men to get divorced," and, second, we need to make it tougher for them to remain single or stray, by "withholding sexual favors until they're married."

These are long-term solutions, and possibly difficult to implement, so we pressed Kathleen Teague (who, in addition to her STOP-ERA affiliation is the executive director of the American Legislative Exchange Council, another New Right institution) for a more immediate solution for women who are poor and single. They should make more of an effort to attract husbands, she told us: "The reason women aren't remarrying is that they don't have the right strategy. . . . Some single women are trying to be martyrs, to prove they can be independent, that they can do anything. It would be better to say, 'How much I'd like to find a nice man!' Many men tell me how turned off they are by women who are trying so hard to be independent."

Abolish Welfare

No one in the New Right, however, is demanding an expansion of welfare payments to cover tuition for "total woman" courses, Freudian psychoanalysis, or other aids to the development of a more demure personality. In fact, as we turn from the New Right's profamily philosophy to their economic programs, the scene changes quickly from images of white-fenced cottages to the gray desolation of crumbling tenements and makeshift rural housing. They believe that welfare should be abolished, for the ostensibly charitable reason that, like other forms of female income, it weakens male responsibility. (George Gilder believes that the expansion of welfare in the 1960s produced "a wreckage of broken lives and families worse than the aftermath of slavery.") Government antidiscrimination efforts should be abandoned. Unions should be weakened. If the right is even partly successful, the future—for women—will look more like Engel's portrait of Manchester in the 1840s than Levittown in the 1950s. For, without the protection of government assistance, the poor assume their historical role as *cheap labor*, and the female poor are cheapest of all—excepting, of course, children.

Consider the trend. In the seventies—beginning at the time that the New Right was still just a gleam in Richard Viguerie's eye— more than a million new women slid into the state of extreme deprivation that the government defines as poverty. They faced, along with the already-poor, a steadily dwindling package of public assistance. Actual dollar value of welfare benefits shrank by 29 percent, nationwide, in the decade of the seventies. Now add the current wave of budget cutbacks. An estimated 15 million women will be directly affected by the cuts in AFDC, Medicaid, food stamps, subsidized school lunches, and dozens of other programs. Many of them will be forced to search for jobs, on or off the books, at any wage. (Ironically, some of Reagan's welfare revisions will decrease the incentive to work—at least on the books—by lowering the welfare payments for every dollar earned. Other welfare cuts, though, are simply throwing women off the rolls.) But the wider effect of the cutbacks, as Frances Fox Piven and Richard Cloward argue in their book, *The New Class War*, will be to drive down the wages of people who are now *above* poverty, because the social programs that have allowed the poor to subsist have also allowed the non-poor to risk pushing for better wages and working conditions.

There is already a sense of desperation among America's female poor—a desperation that translates into a willingness to do almost anything, on any terms. After losing her maintenance job in a Chicago suburb, Janice Cagle said, "I applied for a job in every rinky-dink place I could walk to on foot...give me transportation, and I'll wash toilets." A mother of three, in Brooklyn's Bedford-Stuyvesant area, who asked not to be identified, told us, "If it's a matter of having food on the table, I would do anything short of prostitution." One major effect of Reaganomics, comments Queens College economics professor William Tabb, is "the creation of a veritable army of women who would potentially be available to work under extremely exploitative conditions."

There are still laws to enforce the minimum wage, to protect employees' health and safety and ensure their right to organize—but the right has plans to circumvent them. One idea being promoted by the Heritage Foundation and incorporated in Reagan's economic proposals is for urban "enterprise zones"—designated areas in which companies would be offered tax breaks and other incentives to set up shop. The idea comes, via Margaret Thatcher's administration in England, from Third World countries like Malaysia and the Philippines, where special industrial zones were set up in the 1960s and 1970s to attract multinational corporations. In the Third World models, employers were lured not only by tax holidays and suspension of export duties, but by cheap labor and the absence of health and safety regulations. An estimated 90 percent of the workers in Third World enterprise zones are women, employed chiefly in light assembly work, such as in the manufacture of electronics and garments.

The Enterprise Zone

Supporters of the "enterprise zone" plan include liberals like Congressman Robert Garcia (D.-N.Y.), who believes the zones could attract business to the inner city through tax breaks alone, without offering cut-rate wages. Cornell University professor William Goldsmith, who has just completed a study of enterprise zones, is less sanguine. "So far they're saying they don't want to go below the minimum wage," he told us in a March interview, "but I think that's rhetoric. The idea in England was to create 'little Hong Kongs,' and Hong Kong translates into sweatshops." In case all this sounds remote, the Illinois legislature recently passed a bill that would have allowed industrial zones in which the minimum wage as well as health and safety regulations could have been suspended. (The bill was vetoed by Governor James Thompson in September, 1981.) The kinds of jobs that U.S. enter-

Women perform ⅔ of the world's working hours. Yet they receive only ⅒ of world income & own less than 1% of the world's property

We must act now to end the second class status of women, to reverse male domination, & to destroy stereo-typing.

er... new paragraph.

ROTHCO

prise zones are likely to attract, Goldsmith predicts, are low-paid, light-assembly work that, whether here or in the Third World, is seen as "women's work." At worst, Goldsmith told us, the zones would "serve as vehicles through which an increasingly disenfranchised and desperate group of women could be massively exploited in the labor market."

While liberals debate the value of enterprise zones, the New Right has an even more innovative plan for women: they would like to legalize "homework" so that women could do industrial or clerical work right in their own homes. This was proposed to us as a solution for female poverty by New Right leader Connaught (Connie) Marshner, editor of the *Family Protection Reporter,* staff member of Paul Weyrich's Committee for the Survival of a Free Congress, and chairman of the Pro Family Coalition and of the powerful Library Court, which brings together representatives from various New Right and antifeminist causes for biweekly strategy sessions. "Business and industries should be able to provide jobs that women can do without leaving their homes, like in micro-electronics," she told us.

Unions are justifiably horrified by the idea of a return to homework, which was widespread in the 19th century. Because it would be hidden in private homes and apartments, no wage regulations could be enforced nor would wages have the same meaning as in a normal workplace, since the homeworker would have to cover all the overhead, and probably supply her own sewing machine, typewriter, or other equipment. Worse still, homework could reopen the door to child labor. Near the turn of the century, poor women and their children worked upward of 14 hours a day to fill their piecework quotas in New York City's garment and hat industries. When we raised this possibility to Marshner, she was not dismayed. "I'm not for child labor," she said. "But if the mother had a computer terminal at home and she had a twelve-year-old to help, I'd say, 'why not?' The humanistic reforms of the 19th century made children into economic liabilities." Moral Majority board member Tim La Haye, who shares Marshner's low regard for humanism, is also campaigning for a return to homework. As a result of these proddings from the New Right, the Department of Labor is currently considering loosening its regulations on both homework (which is now banned in seven industries with histories of particularly exploitative practices) and child labor.

A Feminist Program

"Hard times," as one of Avis Parke's nouveau poor friends put it, "have a remarkable way of opening your eyes." The Far Right is on the offensive and—despite polls that show a rapid turn against Reaganomics—liberals have been less than aggressive about presenting their alternatives. And feminists? We wrapped up our research with a new kind of question on our minds: do we, as feminists, have a plan for women?

The question is no longer so redundant, nor the answer as self-evident, as it might once have seemed. Our Movement was born in a time of relative prosperity and economic expansion. Insofar as we had an economic agenda, it was to get into the mainstream and take our chances—or, we hoped, our opportunities—as equals. Equality has been the issue that defined the feminist movement and united women across lines of conventional political affiliation. But now we seem to be faced with the lesson that the black movement learned before us: that legal equality does not guarantee economic survival—and without ERA we will not have even achieved legal equality.

Since our Movement began in the late sixties and early seventies, each recession has bottomed out in a deeper trough; each administration has cut further into that frayed "safety net" of social welfare programs. Men as well as women have seen their aspirations foreclosed and their options narrowed, but after a decade of worsening times, it is women who are left at the bottom. Gender inequality has begun to blur into class inequality, until today even our familiar list of feminist economic reforms—day care, affirmative action, and the more radical demand for equal pay for comparable work—begins to look inadequate to the circumstances.

We need a feminist economic program, and that is no small order. An economic program that speaks to the needs of women will have to address some of the most deep-seated injustices of a business-dominated economy and a male-dominated society. Framing it will take us beyond the familiar consensus defined by the demand for equal rights—to new issues, new problems, and maybe new perspectives. Whether there are debates ahead or collective breakthroughs, they are long overdue: the feminization of poverty demands a *feminist* vision of a just and democratic economy.

"Like all social engineers confronting the failure of their schemes, feminist leaders have refused to acknowledge any responsibility...blaming it instead on 'men' or capitalism."

The Exploitation of Women Is Exaggerated

Allan C. Carlson

Allan C. Carlson is Executive Vice President of The Rockford Institute, a nonprofit center that focuses on the foundations of a free society. The author of numerous articles for scholarly and popular journals, he holds a Ph.D. in European History from Ohio University. The following viewpoint is excerpted from the newsletter *Persuasion at Work* of which Mr. Carlson is editor. Here he examines the changes taking place in the labor market as a result of the increased number of working women.

As you read, consider the following questions:

1. What are the three observations the author suggests that corporation leaders bear in mind?
2. According to the author, what are some of the steps corporations should take in the face of the increasing number of women in the labor market?

Allan C. Carlson, "Women and the Corporation in the Post-E.R.A. Era: One Man's Observations," *Persuasion at Work*, August 1982. Reprinted with permission.

The final and somewhat pathetic demise of the Equal Rights Amendment has left the "Women's Movement" without clear direction, beyond its threats of vengeance. At this point, a glance backward seems appropriate, for the last twenty years have indeed witnessed a major transformation in the roles and, more dramatically, the expectations of American women. Next to the nation's family structure, American business has probably been the most affected by this cultural metamorphosis. The changes in gender-sensitive areas that corporations have absorbed in a relatively brief time have been enormous. Today, certainly, women have entered the management hierarchy and influence the corporate decision-making process to a degree that would have seemed impossible in 1965.

Yet the feminist movement is also sending out signals that American business faces an even rougher road ahead. In the recent Tenth Anniversary issue of *MS.* magazine, for example, Babrara Ehrenreich and Karin Stallard explain that corporations continue to victimize women through automation and plant modernization, purposefully creating low-skilled "dumb" jobs for women at the expense of the higher-paid craft trades that might allow women to improve themselves like male immigrants in the past. "An economic program that speaks to the needs of women," they conclude, "will have to address some of the most deep-seated injustices of a business-dominated economy and a male-dominated society." The current situation, they declare, "demands a *feminist* vision of a just and democratic economy."...

Three Observations

Facing such adamant rhetoric and media-encouraged pressures for renewed and systematic change, corporation leaders might keep a few basic facts in mind:

•*Fundamental, far-reaching and probably irreversible changes in the economic and social roles of women have indeed occurred.*

Significant social evolution is commonly measured in the shift of a few percentage points. The rise in the proportion of women employed in the civilian labor force since 1900 is of an altogether greater magnitude. At the turn of the century, only one of ten married women held paying jobs. By 1950, 24 percent did; by 1970, 41 percent; and by 1980 over half were in the labor market. Among married women, ages 16 to 44, with one or more offspring in school, 40 percent were in the labor market in 1960; two decades later, that figure was 66 percent. For women with children under age six, 45 percent worked in 1980, compared to only 30 percent twenty years earlier.

With this historical fact granted, there are three qualifications that must also be cited. First, as shown above, this massive entry of women into the labor market has proceeded with surprising consistency over the whole of this century, even during the "familial" 1950's. However, it was only briefly during the 1930's and again starting in the late 1960's that this change was rhetorically attached to a feminist ideology.... Rather than being the product of feminist activism, the movement of women into the workplace represents a much more deep-seated and complex historical shift.

Varied Reasons for Working

Second, women have entered the labor force for a variety of reasons. Among the most privileged and best educated, self-fulfillment, ideological necessity or simple boredom are common motivations....Yet for the large majority of working women, economic necessity or the desire to raise their families' standards of living represent the major factor motivating their acceptance of paid labor. For many married women, moreover, such work still represents a supplementary activity to be fitted to the needs of children and home. While nearly half of all women with preschool children now work, it is significant that a slight majority of them fill part-time positions.

Misplaced Blame

Women, like many other allegedly "disadvantaged groups," often blame the private sector for an apparent lack of opportunities, in business and the professions. They look to the government for a solution....As women have sought equality of economic opportunity, they have been persuaded that the only remedy for the obstacles they face is through legislation and even changes in the Constitution. Yet an analysis of the environment facing women shows that far more could be accomplished by eliminating the rules and laws that currently frustrate those women who seek fulfillment in businesses and the professions.

Catherine England and Robert J. Valero, *The Backgrounder*, May 2, 1983. Published by The Heritage Foundation.

Third, while this social transformation has proceeded without significant interruption over the past eighty years, it is difficult to predict the future direction of change. There are, in fact, some indications that the entry of women in the labor market may be reaching some kind of natural limit. Surely, common projections that 80 percent or more of women with preschool children will be working in the year 2000 should be greeted with suspicion. Nor should corporations necessarily build employee compensation and benefit plans around such expectations. Men and women will undoubtedly work out between themselves a variety of family and child-care arrangements defying categorization....

•*There is no single Women's Movement, but there are many*

women's movements....

In truth, the one women's movement heralded in the media as somehow embodying the dreams of all women—i.e., political feminism—represents in style, composition and purpose only one segment of the upper-middle class. And this narrow class orientation has not been without its consequences. Feminists, for example, gleefully participated in bludgeoning the centuries-old cultural mores restraining pre-and extra-marital sexuality and sought repeal of the divorce laws which made the termination of marriage difficult. For women of high income and elite education, such acts could arguably represent a kind of "liberation." But for the large majority of women not so privileged by circumstance, such laws and cultural restraints served to protect—not repress—them from men seeking to evade the responsibilities of marriage and children....

One result of feminist-inspired "liberation" has been the explosive growth since 1960 in the number of female-headed families in the USA and the closely related "feminization of poverty." In recent years, over 150,000 female-headed families have annually fallen below the poverty line, while the number of adult men in poverty has actually declined. If such trends continue, the National Advisory Council on Economic Opportunity recently advised, "the poverty population would be composed solely of women and their children before the year 2000." Yet, like all social engineers confronting the failure of their schemes, feminist leaders have refused to acknowledge any responsibility for this decay—blaming it instead on "men" or capitalism—and have predictably turned to that common panacea for social disruption, the federal budget, urging greater income redistribution in favor of the unmarried mother.

Cultural Pressures

● *Young women are under intense cultural pressures to conform to generally unattainable life goals and commonly expect corporations to provide the magic to make the impossible happen.*

Writing in a recent issue of *Harper's,* Barbara Grizzuti Harrison described her week-long stay at Smith College—the nation's most prestigious women's school and leading recruiting-ground for corporate-bound women—to discover the future of feminism as seen in the expectations of "Smithies" about to enter the business world. She found confused young women expecting brilliant and fulfilling careers, satisfying marriages built on full equality, wonderful yet undemanding children and evenings and weekends devoted to culture and sports; in sum, the archetypal image of women "who have it all" that grace the pages of *MS., Working Woman, Cosmopolitan,* and *Savvy.* "All of these women expect to work," Ms. Harrison writes. "Some of them expect to take time off to have children; others—somewhat naively, perhaps—expect that corporations will provide the flexible work schedule that will enable them to be wives, mothers and career women. For those few with enormous luck, uncommon discipline and large amounts of money, it may work. Most, though, will eventually look to government intervention and corporate paternalism imposed by law to pull it off.

Moreover, the careerism once scorned among men has become a common expectation among many young female executives. Corporations are no longer simply a place to earn a living. In a secularized disoriented age when both faith and family are com-

Allan C. Carlson

151

mon objects of sophisticated ridicule, jobs are increasingly expected to give meaning to an individual's life, to provide an "ultimate purpose" for existence....

Needless to say, business corporations can fulfill neither expectation. Life always involves hard choices and personal sacrifices. No one can have it all. Similarly, while most kinds of work can be fulfilling and rewarding, labor by itself can never fill the cosmic void nor provide an authentic sense of ultimate meaning.

What Can Be Done?

In sum, corporations once again find themselves blamed by radical political forces for cultural dilemmas for which they have no causal responsibility and which they can neither control nor resolve. In the face of such emotion-laden social changes and inflated expectations, the easiest corporate response might be: "Do nothing. There is no reason to try to affect the direction of social change and little that could ultimately be done."

This approach, however, would be shortsighted on both counts. First, the long-term survival of the free enterprise system does depend on the preservation of the modern, two-parent family structure. Born in the crucible of the industrialization process, the modern family sustains the balance between liberty and self-regulated order on which a free society necessarily rests. The family remains the most effective tutor for children in the values necessary to a free economy, such as hard work, self-sacrifice, personal responsibility, delayed gratification and mutual support. Corporate folk wisdom also suggests, correctly I think, that the married employee with a family to feed, house and clothe works harder and exhibits more loyalty to the firm than the unmarried one....

Second, there are positive acts that management might take. They include balanced support for all employees with dependent children. Recognizing the special problems raised by working mothers with small children, corporations might consider the creation of on-site day-care centers, open to the children of employees at a modest fee....

Expand Opportunities

Similarly, companies might consider expanding opportunities for part-time and home work. Significantly, a majority of working mothers with small children express a preference for part-time work, if they can find it. Recent studies have shown part-time workers to be commonly more efficient and productive than their full-time counterparts....

To the degree legally possible, corporations in their hiring and promotion decisions might also give recognition to the special pressures on and needs of the single-income, intact family. What was once the social norm—the family with a working father, full-time mother and small children—finds itself today increasingly at an economic disadvantage relative to the "two-paycheck" couple. Personal sacrifices to raise children, of course, are not necessarily bad nor something for which society must compensate. Yet concrete recognition should be given to the important social role an employee plays as the head of a family.

Finally, in order to protect itself from inflated expectations, management also needs to resist what one critic has called "the totalitarian temptation." While a capitalist economy ultimately depends on the survival of the family, the demands which the former sometimes makes can tend to undermine the latter. After reviewing recent comments by Seagram's Vice President Mary Cunningham concerning the sexual pressures, social tensions and demand for total commitment characterizing many large corporations, the editors of *Fidelity* magazine wrote: "The corporation is faced with a dilemma. Either it will have to become less totalitarian in the claims it makes on workers' lives, or it will have to revert to a workforce which is not only unisex but celibate as well....If the corporation doesn't change..., the first casualty will be the family."

This indictment may be overly harsh, yet it points to the truth that "purpose," "meaning" and the "real work of the world" is found in the creation and sustenance of new human life and its extension into the future. All else, from robotics to high international finance, is but the means to that end. Whatever the silly trappings were that surrounded "the feminine mystique" of the 1950's (and they were many), the women and men who ordered their lives by that informal code at least had an inkling of this deeper truth. Today's challenge is to restate that old verity in terms meaningful to the social and economic realities of the 1980's.

"Of all the strategies that...deal with pay equity for women, the Comparable Worth one does seem to have in it the possibilities...which might allow pay equity without penalizing firms."

An Argument for 'Comparable Worth'

Nancy Barrett

Nancy Barrett is a professor of economics at American University and a former Deputy Assistant Secretary for Economic Policy and Research in the Department of Labor. She has also served on the staff of the Congressional Budget Office. Dr. Barrett has her Ph.D. in economics from Harvard University and was director of the Urban Institute's Program of Research on Women and Family Policy from 1977-1979. She is the author of several books and numerous articles on economic policy, labor markets, and the economic status of women. In the following viewpoint, Dr. Barrett argues that contemporary social justice demands pay equity for women and that the Comparable Worth doctrine can best help achieve that equity.

As you read, consider the following questions:

1. What does the author mean by "pay equity"?
2. What arguments does the author offer against those who claim that higher pay for women would be a disaster for business firms?

Nancy Barrett, "Poverty, Welfare, and Comparable Worth," *A Conference on Comparable Worth, Equal Pay for Unequal Work,* October 17-18, 1983. Published by Eagle Forum Education & Legal Defense Fund, © 1983. Reprinted with permission of the author.

It seems to me that the fundamental issue in Comparable Worth today is not whether or not women's pay ought to be higher or lower than it is, but rather, if one wants to raise women's pay, what is the best way to do it....

The "pay equity" I am going to talk about is whether or not what somebody makes is adequate to support a family, at least at the minimum poverty level. That is, if somebody works full time in paid employment, is that pay enough to support the family? We have heard a lot about the fact that families are really cooperative arrangements between men and women, but the fact of the matter is that all families aren't that way and that, in fact, we have a growing number of families which are headed by women....

The Welfare Dilemma

Twenty-seven percent of all divorced and separated women are on welfare. Half of all black babies in some urban areas, more than half of all black babies, are born out of wedlock. You may say, "Oh, but we aren't really talking about those people." But the problem is we have got this monster out there which is the welfare system....

The problem, of course, in the welfare system is that most of these poor women can't get jobs that pay enough to support their families, and welfare is really a better deal financially for them. The problem is that, if you work 40 hours a week at the minimum wage, you get $140 a week, which isn't a whole lot to live on, even if you have food stamps and other things like that. So, you have millions of people out there who find that welfare is the better alternative to work. Then, you ask that question, "Why is it, then, these jobs pay so little? Why is it that, for so many millions of women, the best that they can do is to find a job at the minimum wage?" This gets back to the question of pay equity, I think....

Female-dominated jobs are in the pink collar ghettos, and I am talking about jobs that are even below the pink collar ghettos such as domestic service. These jobs were structured under the principle of pay equity which assumed that working women were basically either singles who need to support only themselves, or else were married to men who could support them. I am not even talking about social justice here. I am just talking about the general notion that, somehow, people either have to have a living wage, or we are going to be stuck with a system where the government has to subsidize broad categories of people where the labor market isn't paying them enough to get themselves out of poverty....

What Is Social Justice?

The second point which I think is important to take seriously is that our concept of social justice can't be taken as an absolute. Let me see if I can explain what I mean by that. More and more women, for whatever reasons, have been seeking paid employment outside the home and finding that, when they do that, all of this equal opportunity that they hear so much about doesn't seem to be there. There is a growing perception that the system is somehow unfair. Now individuals might reject this idea, but there are a substantial number of people out there who perceive that the system is unfair to women....

People in our society will always disagree on what is just and what is fair and what is not fair; but at least I think that the general public perceives social justice in different ways at different periods and times.

Let me give you an example of this, taking a very classical sort of straw man in the Comparable Worth controversy. That is the question of whether or not nurses are to be paid more than tree trimmers. I don't know whether this ever actually was a true experience, but one example always cited in the Comparable Worth controversy is a case of a hospital that paid the nurses less than it paid the tree trimmers. The nurses were required to have more education, they had more responsibility, they had less convenient working hours; but somehow the male tree trimmers were getting paid more than the nurses. Does this make any sense in the context of contemporary views about social justice?

I can think about a time, not very long ago, maybe a generation or two ago, when most people would have probably thought that discrepancy was fair because, after all, these men have families to

support and they were probably long-time tree trimmers. They had been trimming trees for a long time, whereas these nurses were young girls or spinsters or people who really didn't have any other responsibilities. Why should they get paid as much as these men who had families to support? This is the rationale that many people might have accepted at some time.

I'm saying that people who a generation or two ago might have accepted that rationale may no longer accept it. They now say, "Wait a minute, our concept of social justice has changed; there are other considerations. For example some of these women may actually be supporting families, women may have needs they didn't have before, women are staying in jobs longer, they are having full-time careers, all these things." Some still might think paying the nurses less than the tree trimmers is just, but all I am saying is that the consensus of public perceptions and standards of social justice may have changed, now that we are in a period where lots of women are in the work force. Having said all this, let me get back to what I said I was going to say, and that is talk about Comparable Worth....

Comparable Worth

There is a belief that, if we legislate higher pay in women's jobs, this would be terribly uneconomic and firms would lose a lot of money. Of course, it is possible that could happen, but there is another possibility, certainly a longer run possibility, and that is that these jobs might actually be restructured. There is nothing to suggest that women can't operate high technology. They are doing it right now in offices. We can make women's work a lot more productive than it has been. Some of women's jobs are terribly inefficient in their use of labor because of the fact that women's pay has been quite low, and it hasn't made a whole lot of sense to economize on that labor. We could have a tremendous sort of technological evolution in traditional women's jobs if, in fact, we begin to recognize that pay equity requires that women's pay in these jobs be increased. The market can adjust. The market is terribly resilient. It can adjust to a whole lot of things.

We've heard about unions—these horrible monsters—but, in fact, in union firms productivity is much higher. Why? Not because of the union. Because firms are forced to economize on labor and they do it by getting more capital equipment and organizing work more efficiently. If women's pay went up in secretarial areas and child care, etc., we might, in fact, find that the market adjusted to that by utilizing that labor more efficiently. Meeting the goals of pay equity would mean a productivity gain—wage increases without price increases—because of the fact that women's work in female-dominated occupations would become more productive.

There can be many market outcomes depending on the initial conditions. The market doesn't condition the outcome; rather the initial conditions working with the market do. So, all I can suggest is that, of all the strategies that you can think of to deal with pay equity for women, the Comparable Worth one does seem to have in it the possibilities for technological change and productivity growth which might allow pay equity wihout penalizing firms. I would sugest that we give very serious consideration to the idea that firms that do raise pay for "disadvantaged occupations" get special tax incentives or tax credits for capital equipment that will raise the productivity of these workers. We can't expect firms to swallow these losses; that's crazy....

They would become uncompetitive and go out of business. Rather, what we need to do, as a matter of social justice, is to change the initial conditions to which the market will adjust. We've got to compensate firms that will lose by raising the pay in jobs traditionally held by women, and compensate the firms in a way that will be progressive in the sense of encouraging technological change in the very productivity growth that can allow pay equity.

> *"The equal pay for Comparable Worth*
> *proposal...would be a disaster economically."*

An Argument Against 'Comparable Worth'

Orville V. Bergren

Orville V. Bergren has been the president and spokesman of the Illinois Manufacturers' Association for the past ten years. As the staff director and chief operating officer of the largest state industrial association in the United States, he is a powerful voice for the IMA with its more than 5,500 member firms. Mr. Bergren also has served as secretary-treasurer of the Manufacturers Political Action Committee. In the following viewpoint, he outlines his reasons for believing that "Comparable Worth" legislation would ultimately prove to be economically catastrophic for America.

As you read, consider the following questions:

1. According to Mr. Bergren, what does the case of nurses and nurses' pay demonstrate?
2. In what three ways does the author think private business might be affected by nationwide adoption of the Comparable Worth doctrine?
3. Do you agree with the author? Why or why not?

Orville V. Bergren, "A Business Viewpoint on Comparable Worth," *A Conference on Comparable Worth, Equal Pay for Unequal Work,* October 17-18, 1983. Reprinted with permission.

The concept of equal pay for Comparable Worth is disarmingly attractive on its face, partly because it sounds so fair, and partly because it is so ambiguous that its real meaning and impact do not seem to occur to one without thinking about it. It is being marketed by its proponents under the banner of "pay equity," and who can argue with the principle of "pay equity"?...

Equal pay for Comparable Worth is radically different. It is being pushed on the theory of pay inequity due to alleged discrimination by employers against women as a group. It is based on the theory that certain occupations where women are in substantial majority are significantly underpaid compared to occupations where men are in the majority.

This issue is considerably more complex than the simple sex discrimination basis that its vigorous proponents are claiming. In fact, the issue is not one of sexual discrimination at all. Rather, in having some wages set by government, this doctrine is an assault, whether intended or not, upon our free market economic system, and would result in substantial damage to the U.S. economy....

The Case of Nurses

The fundamental problem of the Comparable Worth doctrine is that it assumes that occupations similar in their demands for knowledge and responsibility will pay equal wages in the absence of discrimination. That is simply not so. The doctrine ignores the fact that there is a market for certain jobs. For whatever reasons, members of certain sexes select certain work. When there are shortages or surpluses of persons to do various jobs, employers will pay differing wages for those jobs.

Consider, for example, the case of nurses and nurses' pay. A few years ago they were underpaid, and a shortage of nurses soon followed. But when that shortage led to increased salaries to appropriate levels, the supply of nurses soon became adequate.

Wage rates reflect the forces of supply and demand in the labor market. There are many variables that enter into the setting of wage rates. Two jobs requiring similar education and responsibility may pay different wages because of the relative attractiveness of the work or work location, or special talents of some kind, or because of the availability of job applicants in a particular field. In other words, all market conditions must be identical to justify equalizing earnings in two occupations.

Of course, the impact of wage contracts negotiated by organized labor unions is an additional factor in wage rates in certain occupations.

The fact is that the well-meaning but misguided doctrine of equal pay for Comparable Worth is simply unworkable. The concepts of wage fairness are entirely subjective—value judgments where the value criteria are not susceptible to being reduced to fair and objective rules. Certainly it is inadequate to say, as does a bill in the Illinois Legislature, that Comparable Worth is "the value of work as measured by the composite of skill, responsibility and working conditions normally required in the performance of work." No matter what kind of point system can be devised to assess the value of a particular job versus another one, it is bound to be inadequate.

Problems of Application

You are the personnel director of a large company. How do you apply Comparable Worth in determining wages in different occupational fields? How do you compare the salary of a well-educated and capable administrative employee with the wage of a unionized, poorly educated but highly productive factory employee to determine their Comparable Worth?

Comparisons among diverse categories such as skilled technicians, machine operators, clericals, truck drivers, food service

Steve Kelley, *The San Diego Union*, reprinted with permission.

personnel, and construction laborers would be required. There are 23,000 occupation titles in the Census Bureau's Classified Index of Industries and Occupations. When one departs from labor marketplace factors in setting wages and salaries, there is deep trouble.

If the doctrine of Comparable Worth is adopted as the law of the land, there is no telling what the end consequences might be. It might not be confined to discrimination based on gender. Why shouldn't a male employee in one occupation complain about the dispartiy in pay in his occupation compared to the pay in other occupational groups? Why shouldn't the hourly production worker making $15,000 per year bring suit to at least double his wages because of his claim that the company president, with his $300,000 annual salary, may be ten times as valuable to the company as the hourly worker, but surely not twenty times? Isn't that pay equity?

If we are talking about intentional discrimination based on sex, let the complainant prove it and enjoy the remedies provided by existing law. If we are talking about "pay equity" based upon subjective valuations of Comparable Worth of different job fields, let us be prepared to take the economic consequences.

Those economic consequences would be great, let there be no mistake about it. Comparable Worth would substantially increase wage costs for many companies. When a U.S. District Court judge recently decreed that Comparable Worth should be the vehicle to overcome what he concluded to be illegal discrimination against women in salaries paid them by their employer, the state of Washington, the judgment was based on Title VII of the U.S. Civil Rights Act. Whether that holds up remains to be seen. It has been estimated that the cost to Washington taxpayers would vary from $300 million to $1 billion, depending upon the mechanism decided upon to ostensibly redress the grievances of the women state employees.

The Costs to Industry

That provides some idea as to the cost to U.S. business if the doctrine were required nationwide and for private employers as well as public. Such increased cost would result in one or more of the following in the private sector:

1. A reduction in the workforce in the affected occupational field....

2. Large companies with employees in many occupational fields could terminate all employees in the affected Comparable Worth field and hire the work done by contract employees of a company specializing in that field—for example, administrative and stenographic work....

3. Increased cost would make a manufacturing company less competitive in international trade.... This is the most ominous prospect of all, because it means loss of jobs for our citizens....

In Summary

The substantially greater wage and salary costs that would result from imposition of the Comparable Worth concept would certainly worsen the already challenging problem that the U.S.

has in international trade competition in manufactured goods.

To summarize:

• The fact that average compensation in some female-dominated occupations is lower than in some male-dominated occupations is not evidence of discrimination against women.

• If in some instances intentional discrimination can be shown, there are already adequate legal remedies available to such women. The average compensation for women is rising significantly compared to men's under present anti-discrimination laws.

• Present compensation variations among occupational groups are the result of myriad forces in the free labor marketplace.

• Comparable Worth is an unworkable idea that would do great damage to our economic system.

• Comparable Worth would surely result in great costs to employers and would, in some instances, hurt lower-qualified women.

• Those higher costs would worsen the ability of the U.S. to compete in the world struggle for industrial jobs.

The concept of equal pay for Comparable Worth is so bad that it is difficult to believe that it is being taken so seriously. It is a highly emotional issue, being exploited by labor unions and women's groups interested in increasing their membership. Alarmingly, many politicians seem to be jumping on the bandwagon, obviously without thinking about the economic impact....

The equal pay for Comparable Worth proposal, attractive as it seems to be politically, would be a disaster economically. It should be rejected.

"[ERA] will do all that is necessary to right the complete wrong that is the injustice of inequality our society practices against women."

The Case for ERA

Cassandra Johnson

Cassandra Johnson is program coordinator for the Department of Human Welfare of the United Methodist General Board of Church and Society. This organization conducts programs of research, education, and action in the areas of environmental justice and survival, human welfare, peace and world order, political and human rights, and social and economic justice. In the following viewpoint, Ms. Johnson argues in favor of ERA claiming that it would represent a major and necessary step in the direction of equality for *all* women.

As you read, consider the following questions:

1. What examples does Ms. Johnson present to illustrate the restricted role of women in America?
2. What arguments does former US Senator Sam Ervin offer in opposition to ERA?
3. How does Ms. Johnson respond to some of the Senator's arguments?

Equal Rights for women is not a new idea. During the First Continental Congress, the wife of John Adams is said to have urged her husband not to disregard equality for women in the drafting of this country's new constitution. Mrs. Adam's advice was not heeded. Most states in the union created laws that hampered a woman's ability to engage in commerce and economic transactions. Married women, particularly, were restricted in participating in even the most fundamental financial arrangements.

Our laws are based upon British common law and at common law both the services and earnings of a wife belong to her husband. For instance, in California in the 1800's a married woman could not contract or make a lease in her own name. In Michigan she could not hire her services out without her husband's explicit permission, nor could she work as bartender unless she was the daughter or wife of the bar owner. Alabama, New York, Oklahoma, and Louisiana, to name only a few, had similar statutes on the books.

The notion of women as incapable of handling even the most rudimentary of commercial transactions was so entrenched in the male psyche that to raise a question to the contrary was considered heresy. Supreme Court Justice Joseph P. Bradley in that court's decision in *Bradwell v. Illinois* (83 U.S. at 141) said:

Man is, or should be, woman's protector and defender. The natural and proper timidity and delicacy which belongs to the female sex evidently unfits it for many of the occupations of civil life. The constitution of the family organization, which is founded in the divine ordinance, as well as in the nature of things, indicated the domestic sphere as that which properly belongs to the domain and functions of womanhood.

Men of the late nineteenth and early twentieth centuries apparently had little knowledge of the "domestic sphere." Cooking, cleaning, laundry, and child rearing are not now, nor have they ever been, synonymous with "delicacy."

Working Outside the Home

Most of these statutes have been repealed or overridden since the beginning of the twentieth century. But the underlying doubt about a woman's ability to function in the world outside of the home has continued. In fact, our society has only recently been forced to recognize that the *necessity* for a woman to function outside the home may be a reality. Even further away from the realm of reality is an admission of the fact that we need an amendment to the US Constitution to ensure unbiased, and therefore equally protective, treatment for women in this country.

Former US Senator Sam Ervin of North Carolina, has written that the Equal Rights Amendment is a document with "revolutionary implications." He argues that the laws enacted for the

Reprinted with permission of the *Minneapolis Star and Tribune*.

"protection" of women's rights are the natural result of the fundamental physiological and functional differences between men and women. He goes on to say:

"Children are God's most helpless creatures. They require years of physical, intellectual, and spiritual nurture to fit them for life as adults.

"To insure that children receive such nurture, customs and laws have created the institution of marriage, and assigned differing legal responsibilities to men and women who marry in respect to themselves, their spouses, and the children they create.

"In assigning these differing legal responsibilities to them, the customs and laws have taken into consideration these things: (1) the circumstance that the husband's role in the creative process is temporary and non-disabling, whereas the wife's role is protracted, arduous, and at least temporarily disabling; and (2) the characteristics and capacities which generally distinguish husbands and wives from each other."

Ervin argues that present laws such as the Equal Pay Act of 1963 and other statutory attempts to eradicate unequal treatment for women in the marketplace are adequate—or becoming adequate—to secure her acquisition of equal opportunity. He also argues that to abolish sexual distinctions in the law would economically harm the married woman, mother, and widow. At present, however, the laws serve to have a severe impact against this very class of people.

Social Security Benefits

The Social Security System was founded in 1936. At that time most women were married, raised children, and generally did not work outside of the home. Divorce was rare. In the ensuing forty-seven years those statistics have changed drastically. Nearly 50 percent of all married women now work outside the home (and the majority of them do so because they *need the money*).

Social Security laws, however, have not changed. Married women who do not work outside the home must depend entirely upon their husband's contributions to the Social Security system for any benefit they receive. The work they do in the home has no monetary value for Social Security purposes, and so they are considered non-contributors. Nevertheless, for many of these homemakers Social Security will provide their *only* source of income in their senior years.

Married women who do work outside of the home contribute to the system on the same percentage basis as their male counterparts. But because women on the national average earn far less than men and have work records that are extensively interrupted by childbirth and rearing, they tend to collect retirement benefits based upon their husband's income and only part of their own contributions. A woman cannot collect her full benefit unless her husband is willing to base his benefit on her contributions.

Divorced women are only entitled to receive dependent benefits based upon an ex-husband's contributions if the marriage lasted at least ten years. Widows under age fifty cannot receive survivors benefits until they are sixty-five.

Many states still have statutes that, in effect, create the legal presumption that the financial assets acquired during a marriage belong to the husband despite the fact that money the wife earned went into the acquisition. Some state statutes will allow the husband to sell mutually-acquired property, such as the family home, without the wife's knowledge or consent. This kind of information is usually not uncovered until a woman becomes personally affected.

Ervin also argues that "the Amendments will nullify all laws of the United States or any state which require husbands to pay alimony to their wives or former wives." This is accurate if the law in question is based upon a notion of protection for females. If, however, the law is based on a notion of marriage as an economic partnership (among other things) alimony awards would be based upon a spouse's contribution to the relationship regardless of her or his sex. Men would not be restricted to paying alimony, but could receive it as well.

Ervin contends that ratification of the E.R.A. will abolish the primary legal resonsibility of fathers to support the children they beget. Actually, both parents are responsible for the support of their children. In reality only 44 percent of divorced mothers are awarded child support payments and only 45 percent of these women are able to collect it on a regular basis.

Differing Treatment Based on Sex

E.R.A. opponents argue that a Constitutional amendment is unnecessary in that there are statutes that currently prohibit discrimination based on gender. Nevertheless, in addition to the state laws that permit property acquired jointly in a marriage to be conveyed exclusively by the husband, the Civil Rights Commission has found 800 different sections of the United States Code alone that require differing treatment based on sex. (The military draft, of course, is included but we should note that there is presently being considered a proposal for legislation to allow for a special category of draftees, i.e.; practicing nurses. Over 90 percent of practicing nurses are women. Being a woman may not always guarantee avoidance of the draft.)

ERA is for Everyone

Statistics released through the Women's Bureau of the U.S. Department of Labor show that 57% of nonwhite women between the ages of 25 and 34 are in the work force; the percentages rise to 60% in the 45-54 age bracket. Absent the clear mandate which would be provided by the passage of the ERA, these women are very vulnerable to the discriminatory practices still prevalent in the job market.

From "The Equal Rights Amendment," a pamphlet published by the National Organization for Women.

Members of the 98th Congress have seen fit to introduce another piece of legislation that would attempt to bridge the inequality gap: The Economic Equity Act. The act provides for changes in the law that would allow a homemaker to establish an Individual Retirement Account in her own right; provide that pensions become a property right in divorce cases; prohibit sex discrimination in all types of insurance; and eliminate certain discriminatory tax provisions.

This act along with the Equal Pay Act and the Equal Credit Opportunity Act of 1975 are all steps in the right direction, but the steps are piecemeal laborious efforts at best. Our society is approaching the question of the denial of equality to women on a per case basis. In comparision the E.R.A. simply reads:

Section 1. Equality of rights under the law shall not be denied or abridged by the United States or by any state on account of sex.

Section 2. The Congress shall have the power to enforce by appropriate legislation, the provisions of this article.

Section 3. This amendment shall take effect two years after the date of ratification.

These three short sentences will do all that is necessary to right the complete wrong that is the injustice of inequality our society practices against women. However, it seems we would rather entwine ourselves in a quagmire of legal doctrine than accept our Christian responsibility and commitment to social justice....

We must come to grips with the kind of injustice experienced by fully one-half of our society—and thereby our entire society—with a system of "special" (read: detrimental) treatment for women.

"ERA proponents have failed to make a case that a constitutional amendment is needed or would provide any constructive benefits to women."

The Case Against ERA

Phyllis Schlafly

Phyllis Schlafly is a conservative political activist who publishes two influential newsletters, *The Phyllis Schlafly Report* and *Eagle Forum Newsletter.* A member of Ronald Reagan's 1980 Defense Advisory Group, she holds a master's degree from Radcliffe College and a law degree from Washington University. Ms. Schlafly is probably best known for her extremely effective campaign against the Equal Rights Amendment. In the following viewpoint, she offers several reasons why she opposes ERA. Although written over 10 years ago, her arguments presented here incorporate principles which have endured as a standard adopted by ERA opponents to this day.

As you read, consider the following questions:

1. Why does the author believe that the subject of the draft "really reveals the hypocrisy of the ERA proponents"?
2. According to the author, what effect would passage of the ERA have upon protective labor legislation?
3. Do you support the ERA? Why or why not?

Phyllis Schlafly, "Let's Stop ERA," *New Guard,* Winter 1983-84. Reprinted with permission.

Many people have naively supported the Equal Rights Amendment because they felt that it would guarantee equal pay for equal work, and improve the status of women in regard to employment. When I debated Congresswoman Martha Griffiths on the Lou Gordon television show, I said that ERA will do absolutely nothing for women in the field of employment. Mrs. Griffiths replied, "I never said it would."

I have testified at 12 state legislative hearings, and in not a single one has a pro-ERA lawyer stated that ERA will do anything whatsoever for women in the field of employment. They know that, in the first place, ERA applied only to Federal and state laws, and not to private employment at all; and secondly, the Equal Employment Opportunity Act of 1972 already guarantees women everything in the field of employment which can be done by legislation.

This law is very specific in regard to hiring, pay and promotions. If any woman thinks she has been discriminated against, she can file her claim with the government, and the government will pay the costs. When AT&T was recently forced to pay $38 million by the Equal Employment Opportunity Commission, this proved that the legislative machinery is fully adequate; the only thing remaining is enforcement.

At the various state legislative hearings around the country, ERA proponents have failed to make a case that a constitutional amendment is needed or would provide any constructive benefits to women. They are still crying around about obsolete discriminations against women which have not existed in the memory of most of us alive today. They are still weeping about women not having the right to vote, women not being able to serve on juries, women not being able to attend college or become lawyers, and other discriminations which disappeared decades ago.

At the ERA hearing in Virginia, the star witness was a 93-year-old woman who said she was an original suffragette and had been campaigning for women's rights since 1909. She concluded her testimony by saying that the proponents of the Equal Rights Amendment have the mentality of 50 years ago, and they are fighting a battle that is long since won. She received a standing ovation.

Drafting Women?

The matter of the draft really reveals the hypocrisy of the ERA proponents. The Equal Rights Amendment will positively make women subject to the draft, and on an equal basis with men. This means running the same obstacle courses, carrying the same 40-50 pound packs, serving in combat and on warships, and all the other dangerous and unpleasant duties. ERA would not permit a system whereby the women would have all the easy desk jobs, with the men assigned to the unpleasant and fighting jobs. ERA

171

would mandate equality across the board.

Most of the ERA proponents are, of course, safely past draft age, a fact which should be kept in mind when they talk so glibly about welcoming the drafting of women. Of the draft-age women who are whooping it up for ERA, most of them—when questioned personally about the draft—hesitate, and then reserve to themselves the right to be a conscientious objector or evade military service in some way.

The ERA proponents say that Congress already has the power to draft women. This is true—but Congress has used this power to exempt women, and that is the way we like it. The overwhelming majority of American men and women do *not* want women drafted, and they don't realize that making women subject to the draft is a precedent-shattering sleeper in ERA.

ERA Is Ineffective

The amendment would transfer from the states to Congress the ultimate legislative power to enact all laws regulating the rights and responsibilities of men and women and the protection of little children, God's most helpless creatures. In addition, the amendment would rob state courts of much jurisdiction by vesting in the Supreme Court supreme power to determine all questions on these subjects.

If ratified, the Equal Rights Amendment would crucify American womanhood on the cross of a dubious, legal equality and a specious legal uniformity.

Sam J. Ervin Jr., *The New York Times*, August 1, 1983.

Anyone who really favors the drafting of women—and there are some—should work for it in the honest, above-board way, that is, by proposing an amendment to the Selective Service Act. Then the issue could be debated and our citizens would know the consequences. The ERA proponents are trying to put over this massive change in our social mores without the majority even realizing what is happening.

ERA proponents also argue that the draft has ended and we will have a volunteer military. It is a very naive person who looks into the future and says, "We are going to have no more wars and no more draft." We are very fortunate that ERA was not ratified 10 years ago, else there would have been thousands of additional tragedies in Vietnam.

The proponents talk about the "benefits" women will receive under the draft. Well, we must also include the "benefits" of being shipped thousands of miles away to fight a jungle war in Southeast Asia, and the "benefits" of being a prisoner of war, and the "benefits" of being missing in action. These are not the kind of "benefits" women want.

The Equal Rights Amendment is like trying to kill a fly with a sledgehammer. You probably won't kill the fly, but you surely will break up some furniture. For example, the laws of every one of our 50 states now make it the obligation of the husband to support his wife and family. This is based on the obvious fact that it is the women who have the babies and, therefore, it should be the men who provide the financial support.

The Equal Rights Amendment will invalidate these state laws in every one of the 50 states because no longer can we have any legislation which imposes an obligation on one sex which it does not impose equally on the other. Removing these state laws will take away from the wife her legal right to be a fulltime wife and mother, supported by her husband.

The result is confirmed by the pro-ERA lawyers who testify at the hearings. They admit that they do want to remove the full obligation of the husband and make the obligation for financial support of the family fall *equally* on the husband *and* the wife. Such a legalistic equality would impose a realistic double burden on the wife, because she is still the one who will have the babies.

Labor Legislation

A third area of concern is the matter of protective labor legislation. Women who work in industry are protected by many laws, provisions in union contracts, and company policies which guarantee their right to be treated like a woman. The Equal Rights Amendment will wipe these all out, and the proponents say this is what they want.

A woman can compete equally with a man in intellectual, professional, and academic occupations because women are just as smart as men. However, a woman can*not* compete equally with a man in manual labor or in physical work because she is *not* as strong. Anyone who doubts this truism should look at the Olympic Games. If the men and women competed with each other in the Olympics, the women would simply not win any gold, silver or bronze medals.

The fourth area is Social Security. When a working woman retires, she now receives a higher financial payment than a man who has worked the same number of years at the same salary. All preferential treatment for women would be wiped out by the Equal Rights Amendment.

Hayden Modification

During most of the time that the Equal Rights Amendment was in Congress, and during the time when many prominent people became committed to the Equal Rights Amendment, it had attached to it another clause called the Hayden Modification which

173

Phyllis Schlafly

read, "The provisions of this Article shall not be construed to impair any rights, benefits or exemptions conferred by law upon persons of the female sex."

This clause was struck out under agitation from the women's liberationists. It shows very clearly that the effect of the Equal Rights Amendment would be precisely to deprive wives of the *right* to be supported by their husband, of the *benefits* that working women have under protective labor legislation and Social Security, and of the *exemption* that draft-age girls have from the military.

There is another section of ERA called Section 2 which shifts to Congress the power to implement the Equal Rights Amendment by appropriate legislation. This is a grab for power at the federal level, pure and simple. It will remove from the state legislatures, the bodies closest to the will of the people, the authority to legislate in the entire field of women's rights, including criminal law, property rights or anything pertaining to domestic relations. All this will be transferred out of the hands of the state legislatures and into the hands of Congress, the executive branch, and the federal courts.

Proponents' Tactics

Unable to answer the arguments about the rights women now posess which they will lose if ERA is ratified, the ERA proponents have shifted their tactics. Time and time again, instead of trying to make an affirmative case for ERA, the proponents resort to abusing their opponents. One of their favorite tactics is to accuse the opponents of being financed by a giant conspiracy made up of the Communist Party, the Ku Klux Klan, the AFL-CIO, the John Birch Society, and the Catholic and Mormon Churches. The ridiculousness of this charge is self-evident. One wag suggested that anyone who could get all those groups together ought to be nominated for the Nobel Peace Prize!

Another tactic is to argue that, since ERA passed Congress by very large majorities, it must deserve our support. In essence, this argument is, Big Brother in Washington, D.C. knows best.

The fact is that the story is now leaking out as to why some of the senators and congressmen voted for the Equal Rights Amendment a year ago. One prominent senator frankly admitted to his constituents that he voted for it only "to get those militant women off my back." Another well-known senator said he voted for it because of "sheer terror."

A third prominent senator said he knew it was a piece of bad legislation, but voted for it anyway. Congress' passage of ERA was a classic case of buckpassing to the state legislatures.

Having failed to demonstrate any legal rights which women will gain through ERA, the proponents have fallen back on the argument that it is "symbolic" and needed for "psychological" objectives. But the United States Constitution should not be turned into an instrument to provide a psychological cure for personal problems.

The first dozen states that ratified the ERA did so without hearings or debate. They just called it up and passed it because they thought it was what women wanted. Now, the legislators are having second thoughts. One-third of the states that ratified ERA in 1972 are considering motions to rescind. On March 15, 1973, the Nebraska Legislature rescinded its earlier ratification of the Equal Rights Amendment. When Alabama on June 12, 1973 voted

26 to 6 to reject ERA, it became the 20th state to reject the Equal Rights Amendment.

The ERA proponents have promised to continue the fight for six more years, but we hope the state legislators will not be stampeded into accepting an amendment which, like Prohibition, they will surely regret.

Distinguishing Between Fact and Opinion

This activity is designed to help develop the basic reading and thinking skill of distinguishing between fact and opinion. Consider the following statement as an example. "Two out of three adults who fall into the federal definition of poverty are women." This statement is a fact with which few women, men, or government officials would disagree. But consider a statement which attributes female poverty to male domination. "Women remain poor because men continue to hold the positions of power and refuse to promote and increase the wages of their female employees." Such a statement is clearly an expressed opinion. A woman in a frustrating, dead-end job may agree with this statement, but to a male manager who treats his female and male employees equally, the statement is an outright attack.

When investigating controversial issues it is important that one be able to distinguish between statements of fact and statements of opinion.

The following statements are taken from the viewpoints in this chapter. Consider each statement carefully. *Mark O for any statement you feel is an opinion or interpretation of facts. Mark F for any statement you believe is a fact.*

If you are doing this activity as a member of a class or group, compare your answers with those of other class or group members. Be able to defend your answers. You may discover that others will come to different conclusions than you. Listening to the reasons others present for their answers may give you valuable insights in distinguishing between fact and opinion.

If you are reading this book alone, ask others if they agree with your answers. You too will find this interaction very valuable.

O = *opinion*
F = *fact*

177

1. The poor take the brunt of federal budget cuts.
2. Two out of three adults who fall into the federal definition of poverty are women.
3. The only thing that holds some women back is a sub-normal supply of assertiveness.
4. Between 1978 and 1980 the number of women who head households who became poverty statistics rose to 150,000 per year.
5. The ERA is the only way to achieve legal equality for women.
6. Fundamental, far reaching, and probably irreversible changes in economic and social roles of women have occurred.
7. At the turn of the century, only one of ten married women held paying jobs.
8. Economic necessity, not feminism, represents the major factor motivating most women's acceptance of paid labor.
9. One result of feminist-inspired "liberation" has been the growth in the number of poor, female-headed families.
10. Young women are under intense cultural pressure to conform to unattainable life goals and expect corporations to provide the magic to make the impossible happen.
11. Corporations will need to make significant changes in order to incorporate working mothers on a large scale.
12. Twenty-seven percent of all divorced and separated women are on welfare.
13. Half of all black babies are born out of wedlock.
14. Most poor women can't get jobs that pay enough to support their families, and welfare is a better deal for them.
15. All people must have a living wage or we will be stuck with a system where the government has to subsidize people who don't.
16. Paying nurses less than tree trimmers is unjust.
17. Comparable worth is an assault on our free-market economic system.
18. For whatever reasons, members of certain sexes select certain work.
19. Wage rates partly reflect the forces of supply and demand in the labor market.

Periodical Bibliography

The following list of periodical articles deals with the subject matter of this chapter.

Mona Charen — "The Feminist Mistake," *National Review*, March 23, 1984.

Geoffrey Cowley — "Comparable Worth: Another Terrible Idea," *The Washington Monthly*, January 1984.

Barbara Ehrenreich & Frances Fox Piven — "The Feminization of Poverty," *Dissent*, Spring 1984.

Forbes — "A Pernicious, Destructive Idea," January 16, 1984.

Ted Gest — "Battle of the Sexes over Comparable Worth," *U.S. News & World Report*, February 20, 1984.

Inquiry — "The Worth of Women's Work," December 1983.

Jake Lamar — "A Worthy but Knotty Question," *Time*, February 6, 1984.

Elizabeth Marsis & Richard Moore — "What's a Woman's Work Worth?" *The Progressive*, December 1983.

Abigail McCarthy — "Facing the Facts: The Economics of Women," *Commonweal*, March 23, 1984.

Lincoln C. Oliphant — "Toward a New ERA?" *National Review*, June 24, 1984.

Patricia O'Toole — "Sex and Your Salary," *Vogue*, September 1983.

Diana M. Pearce — "The Feminization of Ghetto Poverty," *Society*, November/December 1983.

Jane Bryant Quinn — "Comparable Pay for Women," *Newsweek*, January 16, 1984.

Lisa Schiffren — "The Return of the ERA," *Inquiry*, June 1984.

Peggy Simpson — "The Fight for Pay Equity," *Working Woman*, April 1983.

Time — "How Long Till Equality?" July 12, 1982.

Howard B. Tolley Jr. — "Challenging Discriminatory Wages for Women's Work," *USA Today*, May 1983.

Organizations to Contact

The editors have compiled the following list of organizations which are concerned with the issues debated in this book. All of them have publications or information available for interested readers. The descriptions are derived from materials provided by the organizations themselves.

American Association for Affirmative Action
President D. Robert Ethridge
Emory University, 301 Admin. Bldg.
Atlanta, GA 30307
404-329-6017

The AAAA is a group of Equal Opportunity and Affirmative Action officers united to foster the implementation of affirmative action and equal opportunity and provide a liaison with federal, state, and local agencies involved with equal opportunity compliance. The organization publishes a quarterly newsletter.

American Civil Liberties Union
132 S. 43rd St.
New York, NY 10036
212-944-9800

The ACLU champions the rights of man set forth in the Declaration of Independence and the Constitution. It has worked for minority, poor, and women's rights. It publishes a variety of newsletters and research works.

Center for Community Change
1000 Wisconsin Ave. NW
Washington, DC 20007
202-342-0519

The group assists community groups of urban and rural poor in making positive changes in their communities. The organization lends technical assistance to communities and works to make government more responsive to the needs of the poor. It publishes newsletters and citizen action guides.

Center for Women Policy Studies
2000 P. St. NW, Suite 508
Washington, DC 20036
202-872-1770

The organization's purpose is to educate the public regarding changes in the legal and economic status of women by conducting studies of credit discrimination against women, occupational segregation, sex discrimination, and sexual assault. It publishes newsletters, reports, articles, papers, and books.

Citizens' Committee for Immigration Reform
1424 16th St. NW, 4th Fl
Washington, DC 20036
202-331-1759

This committee of national leaders is interested in the reform of US immigration and refugee policy. The group proposes to legalize a majority of undocumented aliens and distributes immigration information. It publishes a monthly newsletter.

Commission for Racial Justice
105 Madison Avenue
New York, NY 10016
212-683-5656

The commission's purpose is to make racial justice a reality in our national life. It publishes a variety of newsletters.

Eagle Forum
Box 618
Alton, IL 62002
618-462-5415

The organization opposes the ERA because it is inconsistent with the rights of women and families.It publishes a monthly newsletter.

Equal Employment Advisory Council
1015 15th St. NW
Washington, DC 20005
202-789-8550

The organization promotes and presents the interests of employers and the public regarding employment guidelines in equal opportunity employment practices.It publishes books and monographs.

ERA Impact Project
c/o NOW Legal Defense and Education Fund
132 W. 43rd St.
New York, NY 10036
212-354-1225

The organization serves as a national information clearinghouse on state ERA legislation.

Federation for American Immigration Reform (FAIR)
1424 16th Street NW, Suite 701
Washington, DC 20036
202-328-7004

The group advocates comprehensive reform of present immigration laws and promotes enforcement of laws against illegal immigration. The Federation seeks to establish a single, stable ceiling for all legal immigration. It sponsors seminars and publishes a monograph series.

Food Research and Action Center
1319 F. St. NW, 5th Fl.
Washington, DC 20004
202-452-8250

The organization's purpose is to render legal assistance as well as non-legal research and community organizing assistance to poor people's organizations to make the federal food assistance programs more responsive to the acute needs of millions of hungry Americans. The Center publishes pamphlets, research, and guides.

Moral Majority
305 Sixth St.
Lynchburg, VA 24504
804-528-0070

This organization is a political movement founded by Rev. Jerry Falwell that is dedicated to convincing morally conservative Americans that it is their duty to register and vote for candidates who agree with their moral principles. The organization claims a membership of 72,000 and publishes a monthly newspaper.

MS. Foundation for Women
370 Lexington Ave.
New York, NY 10017
212-689-3475

The organization's goals are to eliminate sex discrimination and to improve the status of women and children in society. The foundation publishes *Ms.* magazine and an annual report.

National Association for the Advancement of Colored People
186 Remsen St.
Brooklyn, NY 11201
212-858-0800

The organization's purpose is to achieve equal rights through the democratic process and eliminate racial prejudice for all American citizens by removing racial discrimination in housing, employment, voting, schools, the courts, and others. The association publishes a variety of newsletters, books, and pamphlets.

National Association for the Advancement of White People
Box 10625
New Orleans, LA 70181
504-831-6986

The organization wants to promote equal rights for all, including white people; stop "so-called" affirmative action, busing and anti-white racism on television and in film; limit immigration; reform welfare programs; and preserve the heritage and advance the interests of whites. The association publishes a monthly newsletter.

National Association of Working Women
9 to 5
1224 Huron Rd.
Cleveland, OH 44115
216-566-9308

The organization seeks to help build local office worker organizations to fight sex and race discrimination on the job. It supports equal opportunity hiring and publishes a monthly newsletter.

National Committee on Pay Equity
1201 16th St. NW, Rm 615
Washington, DC 20036
202-822-7304

The committee's goal is to raise wages for jobs held predominantly by females. It publishes briefing papers and conducts conferences.

National Immigration Project of the National Lawyers Guild
14 Beacon St., Suite 407
Boston, MA 02108
617-227-9727

This organization is a group of lawyers, law students, and legal workers that educates and organizes for progressive immigration. The organization publishes newsletters and maintains a speakers bureau.

National Organization for Women
425 13th St. NW, Suite 723
Washington, DC 20004
202-347-2279

NOW is an organization of men and women who support full equality for women in truly equal partnership with men. NOW acts to end prejudice and discrimination against women, supports the ERA and investigates the causes for the feminization of poverty. The group publishes monthly newsletters.

National Urban League
500 E. 62nd St.
New York, NY 10021
212-310-9000

The league aims to eliminate racial segregation and discrimination in the United States and to help black citizens and other economically and socially disadvantaged groups to share equally in every aspect of American life. The organization publishes newsletters, reports and surveys, and magazines.

Potomac Institute
1501 18th St. NW
Washington, DC 20036
202-332-5566

The organization is concerned with developing human resources by expanding opportunities for racial and economically deprived minorities. One of the group's purposes is to provide programs to increase opportunities for minorities.

Rav Tov International Jewish Rescue Organization
125 Heyward St.
Brooklyn, NY 11206
212-875-8300

The organization aids people who wish to immigrate to the US or other Western countries and provides financial assistance to immigrants in conjunction with the State Department. The group assists with visas and housing and provides moral support. Its publications include newsletters and reports.

US-Mexico Border Program
1501 Cherry St.
Philadelphia, PA 19102
215-241-7132

The Program promotes public understanding of the nature and causes of the problems along the Mexico-US border, especially concerning Mexican migration to the US. The program also defends the working rights of undocumented immigrants. The program is part of a project by the American Friends Service Committee and publishes a newsletter twice a year as well as research papers, statements, and testimonies.

Wider Opportunities for Women
1325 G. St. NW, Lower Level
Washington, DC 20005
202-638-3143

The organization's purpose is to expand employment opportunities for women. Its focus is to recognize the need for compensatory training and education to remedy deficiencies resulting from sex discrimination and stereotyping. The organization provides career counseling, access to non-traditional jobs, skills training, job development and placement, and employment advocacy. It publishes a number of newsletters, books and directories.

Women's Equity Action League
805 15th St. NW, Suite 822
Washington, DC 20005
202-638-1961

The league's purpose is to secure legal and economic rights for women. Its focus is the economic problems of aging women and discrimination in employment and education. The League publishes a variety of reports and action kits.

Working Group on Domestic Hunger and Poverty
475 Riverside Dr., Rm 572
New York, NY 10115
212-870-2307

The group aids in the organization of anti-hunger coalitions throughout the US and compiles nationwide statistics on federal budget cuts and poverty needs. It publishes newsletters and research.

Bibliography of Books

Ken Auletta — *The Underclass.* New York: Random House, 1982.

Judith Bentley — *American Immigration Today.* New York: Julian Messner, 1981.

David Carlenir — *The Rights of Aliens.* New York: Avon Books, 1977.

Barry Chiswick, ed. — *The Gateway: US Immigration.* Washington D.C.: American Enterprise Institute for Public Policy, 1982.

John Crewdon — *The Tarnished Door.* New York: New York Times Book Co., Inc., 1983.

Terry Easland and William J. Bennett — *Counting By Race.* New York: Basic Books Inc., 1979.

Nathan Glazer — *Affirmative Discrimination.* New York: Basic Books, Inc., 1975.

Barry Gross — *Discrimination in Reverse: Is Turnabout Fair Play?* New York: New York University Press, 1978.

Grace Halsell — *The Illegals.* New York: Stein and Day, 1978.

Robert B. Hill — *The Illusion of Black Progress.* Washington, D.C.: National Urban League, 1978.

Leo Kanowitz — *Equal Rights: The Male Stake.* Albuquerque: University of New Mexico Press, 1981.

Burton M. Leiser — *Values in Conflict: Life, Liberty, and the Rule of Law.* New York: Macmillan Publishing Co., Inc., 1981.

Sasha C. Lewis — *Slave Trade Today.* Boston: Beacon Press, 1979.

Demetrios G. Papademetiou and Mark J. Miller, eds. — *The Unavoidable Issue: US Immigration Policy In the 1980s.* Philadelphia: Institute for the Study of Human Issues, 1983.

William Ryan — *Equality.* New York: Pantheon Books, 1981.

Thomas Sowell — *Race and Economics.* New York: David McKay Company, Inc., 1975.

Leonard A. Valverde, ed. — *Bilingual Education for Latinos.* Washington: Association for Supervision and Curriculum Development, 1978.

Marjorie P.K. Weiser

Ethnic America. New York: The H.W. Wilson Company, 1978.

Walter E. Williams

The State Against Blacks. New York: New Press-McGraw Hill Book Company, 1982.

J. Alan Winter, ed.

The Poor: A Culture of Poverty or a Poverty of Culture. Grand Rapids: William B. Erdmans.

The Women's Labor Project of the National Lawyers Guild

Bargaining For Equality. San Francisco: The Women's Labor Project, 1981.

Anne Wortham

The Other Side of Racism. Columbus: Ohio State University Press, 1981.

Index

190